A DAUGHTER'S LATITUDE

A Daughter's Latitude

NEW & SELECTED POEMS

Karen Swenson

For David –
     a son with his
own latitude.
     My best,
     Karen Swenson

10/13/93

COPPER CANYON PRESS
Port Townsend, Washington

Copper Canyon Press acknowledges and thanks Gray Foster, for the use of her painting *Kannon* (oil and rice paper on wood), on the cover.

The publication of this book was supported by grants from the Lannan Foundation, the National Endowment for the Arts, and the Washington State Arts Commission. Additional support was received from Elliott Bay Book Company, Cynthia Hartwig, and the many members who joined the Friends of Copper Canyon Press campaign. Copper Canyon Press is in residence with Centrum at Fort Worden State Park.

LIBRARY OF CONGRESS CATALOGING-IN-PUBLICATION DATA

Swenson, Karen, 1936–
A daughter's latitude: new & selected poems / Karen Swenson.
Port Townsend, WA: Copper Canyon Press, c 1999.
p.   cm.
PS3569.W39D38   1999
811/.54 21
ISBN 1556590946 (alk. paper)

99-006015
CIP

9 8 7 6 5 4 3 2 FIRST PRINTING

COPPER CANYON PRESS
Post Office Box 271
Port Townsend, Washington 98368

CONTENTS

The Nineteen Sixties

from AN ATTIC OF IDEALS

Part I

Part II

The Nineteen Seventies

from EAST-WEST

The Nineteen Eighties

The Nineteen Nineties

This book has been arranged to include poems uncollected in book form, from my early years as a poet to the present, as well as poems from previous books. The uncollected poems have been included at the beginning of each dated section.

    – K.S.

A DAUGHTER'S LATITUDE

The Nineteen Sixties

Plato's Cave

Blood is red. They say napalm
snarls yellow and crimson
through the buckram palm leaves,
but the fire is at my back.

I am watching shadows funneled into a tube,
war neat in a box, canned as concentrated juice.
The soldiers march newsprint faces through
landscape indecisive between black and white.
Dots swarm the graph lines of the screen,
pepper and salt clotting to grenades and rice
in a monochrome entertainment of death.

Could this ashed drama be wrenched out
to the dimension of my hand?
Listen. Someone is crying
in the fire a day before my eyes.

Cooper Square

A mother on Long Island buys her son
heroin out of her household money, puts
it on the list between coffee and lightbulbs
and counts her rosary at night.

Manhattan has gone back to beads.
They necklace the cube in Cooper Square.
Daddy's strung-out seeds in Manhattan's labyrinth
become an indeterminate disease of initials, OD and DOA.

On 105th St. an OD waits to become a DOA
in the brick-and-broken-bottle sun.
The children park their bicycles to pick his pockets.
The old woman in the liquor store calls the cops.

Experimenting with their own chemistry
the flower children, all their petals blown,
lean hungry under the cube in Cooper Square
and beg beyond all affluence.

Night Cry

The radiator taps like a frantic blind man.
Do not weep in the night. Please. Do not cry.
Some dread lies furtive between blocks and clay –
my sparrow heart, tell me that I too may sleep,

but you only draw my hand against your face.
Five stones into the river's current
you know I am no shield
against the cat claw of dream.
I will only say it is not true,
and you are uninterested in candied placebos.

You release my hand. Allowing me to retreat,
fatuous as my flowered robe, to my own darkness.
You send my wraith to bed uncomforted,
a crocheted cap for a stillborn baby.

Office Party: Distaff View

My mind is in the deep freeze
wrapped in airtight plastic,
and who would want my thoughts
even glossed by hollandaise?

I have left my face with the baby-sitter
and come here sketched in eyebrow pencil,
hesitant as a dress in basting stitches,
to stand beside my husband – my name tag –
and watch the shrimp pass by, boiled commas
nodding at the edge of a crystal bowl.

The accountant's wife splutters freckles between
the pink-bowed lattice of her open-backed gown.
Ambition, a pulled tendon, aches through conversations.
And I, trying to make jelly-glass gestures into Dresden,
am an extra, an appendix, my function organized out.

Take me home, husband, and we'll make
love on the oriental rug, laying
a little ontology on another pattern
stylized beyond reality.

FROM *An Attic of Ideals*

PART I

The Heroines

The heroines lived with their husbands'
shelved principles
in an attic of ideals,
kept dusted the broken bowls of justice, honor,
all men hold the best
and kept in the quiet reservoir of womanhood,
a still lake where
they leaned from the shore and saw
not their faces but their faith,
because what you cannot be
must still belong to you.

The heroines kept the attics clean
because they believed
the attic was Nirvana,
that man could alchemize them into inexistence,
but they were only caretakers,
dusters of undone deeds,
only ladies adrift in the lake.
Ophelia, innocence offended, sang bawdy songs
and drowned in the attic.

Virginia

First they took off one breast
then the other
then her ovaries came out
then her pituitary gland.

Slowly they dismembered her
to keep her alive.
They started with the things they understood
cutting her womanhood away,
the most obviously infected part,
and then the module
whose function they weren't sure of.
It is a matter of taking out the fuse
so the lights won't go on.

She stands on the corner and talks to me,
wearing her scars behind the soft sculpture of foam,
tells me that living with death is not too bad.
It gives life salt, not depending
on any other time to make up your tense,
and days become what they always should have
been, pungent with the present.

She leaves me to go to the hospital,
moving from biopsy to biopsy
as they cut her back to the bone,
but the more they minus
the more multiples there are.

Dear Elizabeth:

We are almost all homely,
beauty being rare as a round stone,
and I was once homelier than thou,
      pocked teeth, long nose, plain geometry jaw,
      an unleavened matzo angling down the street,
      pigeon-toed strip of bespectacled lath.
The swan's story is a sweet one,
but it is a puffball beast.
Robins, April-pretty, live on worms
to become unnoticeable by June.
      But the hatched hawk, gall-eyed
      in clumsy fluff between feet and beak,
      lives on fought flesh – waiting
      for shoulders to lean upon the wind.
I tell you this to keep comfort till your time.
A man is held stronger by beauty he knows
than any loveliness his eye can see.
      And don't mind Helen with Grecian ships,
      that is the male's most fervent legend,
      told by a wanderer totally blind.

For Elizabeth Difiore

The Barmaid and the Alexandrite

Route 66, a rut of scenery and cigarettes –
all I know of Indianapolis
is a ladies' room at 3 AM.

I slept with strangers.
The mornings, born green,
were honed down by the sun

to my cigarette –
one spark on the night window

as the telephone pole tally
ticked down to Flagstaff,
a bed, a bath, a bar and there

her round arms, pale,
moonlit adobe dreams,
passed the beers down the bar.

With a smile like a torn billboard
she moved through male voices
from Tucumcari, to Gallup, to Flagstaff.

Desert towns isolated on the land, bright and brittle,
as a potato-chip bag caught on a cactus.

The night slackened to a shade of New York City snow
and the last pair of cowboy boots measure
their metronome stride on the dew-darkened sidewalk.

Stirring her coffee she talked –
boardinghouses, suitcases,
wild daisies wilting in a peanut-butter jar.

And then she reached into her bra,
undid a safety pin, and set in my hand
the ring, a welt of color warm from her skin –

an alexandrite, heliotrope-heavy in the half-light.
Two women in the dirty-laundry dawn
hunched over a stone.

Silence circled from the cold desert
to slither the edge of our skirts.

We watched the stone waver in the mizzling sun
as its color curdled to green in my hand –
jelled green in the first sparrow call.

I left on the bus to find my way back
home – the honeycomb that fits you into all its holes –
gnawed my way back through hamburgers

and the anonymous arteries of America
trying to read answers in road signs.

And she passed out the beers
wearing a stone against her breast –
a dark bruise that she watched

resolve again to green in every dawn
from Telluride, to Taos, to Galisteo.

The Quilt

Alive in a brown stucco house
picketed by thorns of a barberry hedge
(in fall their berries spattered red
as a smashed Christmas ball)

she sat at the front window in
a horsehair rocker sleek as
the bottoms of her pots and pans.

She hated as she dug the needle
into the widening pattern of the quilt –
a patchwork of her deciduous dresses

radiating from the center of satin,
white stone cast first.
The memories of material
spread their circles around it.

A swatch of evening dress never worn.
A rectangle of the coat she made herself.
She pinned them and pierced them,

fettering the failures together
with a tense silk thread,
cross stitch, blanket stitch, chain stitch,

her embroidery precise as the steel shaft.
When the design was updated by
the lining of her worn-out suit,
she smoothed the quilt across their bed.

Hooks and Eyes

Irish lace and linen –
she had the design right,
the skirt's mountain-laurel pucker,
but no hooks and eyes.

So she sewed me in,
a last-minute needle
through my first communion –
my marriage to Christ.

The next time it was Grandma's
pale wedding gown,
a supple splurge of curdled satin.

Her damned needle basted me in again,
a lean noose loop.
Through a succession of dresses
her loose stitch has pulled

pattern and fabric to the scissor's mouth.
Only now I realize
that's what she's always done;
gathered me into the paradigm, a slack abstract.

I bend my coffin cloth of flesh
basted hem to skin.
She's forgotten the hooks and eyes
again, and sewed me in.

PART II

The Moon

Their footprints on her face –
you could tell they enjoyed marking her up.

I have seen my son the same,
a joy of sloshing galoshes
across a brisk sheen of new snow.

It's something in the male;
they can't stand just openness.

They have to put things into it –
a flag, a rocket, a foot,
any signature of their spore.

Being female, I felt sorry for her.
Not that it will make any difference

to lovers and harvests and I do realize
we may need her some day, a stepping stone
for some new hypocrisy of hope

as we put distance between ourselves
and our latest botch of civilization.

But did the deflowering have to
be so public? Did we have to wave
the bloodied sheet? Columbus was kinder.

This is a very female point of view,
I realize, foolish, even sentimental.

But it hurt, woman to woman,
to see their footprints on her face,
for women are, after all, only space.

Woman: Gallup, NM

The shadow of her profile lay stringent
across the step of curb,
a styptic etch against his blood,

and he silent beside her,
lesions pale in the scars
of his limp hands.

The baby against
the breathing of her breast
watched, with black eyes
from under a ruffled lambchop hat,

the bus passengers walk
arranged oblivion in and out.

They did not talk.
She yielded him nothing but rigid back;
her neck a carved anger of tendons
where the black down murmured.

God! what had he done
that could not be darned with tears?

She sat lizard dry.
Road and railroad ran through her head.
The land ate red
to a frail mirage of mountains.

He raised his head
and with a gentleness of hand,

hesitant as settling dust,
stroked the curve of her neck.

His motion was only man to woman.
It was not enough.
Her silhouette, knifed out of sunlight,
fell into the gutter.

The passengers walked over it,
and she was mute as snakeskin.

If he had cast himself into his own
shadow under the bus wheel
she would not have wept
or cracked her parched profile,

until night erased it
or the baby gummed a pale cry.
He reached out again,
a cramped consent of fingers
down her shoulder.

His arm, opening
to press the baby's head against
the hollow of her collarbone,
scythed back into his breath.

Across a red scorch to mountains
she shattered on the pavement.

The Price of Women

Every woman, you say, has her price:
a house with trees and tricycles,
a yellow porcelain sink that matches
shine to shine the kitchen cabinets,

and some are more expensive
requiring Tiffany's and other labels
draped over their luncheon chairs.

These are the bargains of love
or quiet or just another body to be by.

But are they? Isn't this the way we
counter what we will not give, a game
of poker-chip exchange – an emerald for
emotion, not an equal sign

but the ellipse of instead of –
because what would I do if
you or anyone walked into the room

in the middle of the commercial
and asked for my life?

Farewell to Fargo: Selling the House

Olivia is dying. Bring your best black dress.
There will be nothing to take back.
The red squirrels gnawed into all the trunks
and devoured everything in the attic.

The summons was rescinded. She still lives.
I have been called to a different funeral.

An ebony elephant. A china invalid's cup,
blue-and-white, fragile as the tremor of veins
warping an old hand. The dining-room table
that curves into clawed brass feet.

Little heaps of leftovers under plastic,
they stand isolated,
punctuation marks without our sentence.

The purchasers walk between them,
choosing what they will reincarnate.
I cannot bear the helplessness
of the objects dying from our lives.

Aimless as a mourner dismissed from the grave,
I wander out to the garage.
I climb the stairs to the loft.
There is a raw sound of scampering
in the dust before my footfalls.

I find Ferd's silver-capped cane
behind the lawn mower.

He died when I was in the second grade,
a fat man in a gilt frame.

Six daughters and two sons divisible
into workers, the greedy, and dreamers.

Ferd and Peter kept the store.
Olivia kept the books.
Elizabeth kept the house.

Ann painted roses on china
and grapes on canvas.
Claire, in a purple velvet gown,
played a gold harp.

Julia and Amelia moved after
the quarrel across town and
were only asked to funerals.

They've all gone to the wall, photographs,
leg-of-mutton sleeves
leaning on the porch rail.
Watch chains linked like beaded portieres.

There were rides on Sunday after mass,
parasols behind horses.
Sun-honed light above the wheat.

The prairie dust silted into every ruffle.
Then they trotted back to town,
to the house harrowed between the trees,
to dinner on the mahogany table,

eating out of the shine of their faces
while the Red River, a block away,
gnawed its banks roiling northward.

And what did they ride out to see? There is no
tree, no shrub, no rise of land on the plain.

One by one, they died upstairs
under the great arm of the elm
and were taken down in narrow chests,
bumping the turn of the banister.

Now only one remains, her mind
sieved by the years to pabulum, waiting
to be a name laid into the grass.
She does not know the house is sold.

I take the cane back to the house and
lay it on the dining-room table to be bought.

The purchasers are gone.
There is a storm coming.
I stand on the front step.

The elms hover over the emptied house.
Seeds snow down against the dark sky,
platelets spiraling in a quickening breeze.

Red squirrels on the roof quarrel
in the fevering silence. Chain lightning
shocks heaven into a jigsaw.

The screen door behind me screams
its spring and slams.

Nursing Home

THE CANARY

In this hospital odor
his wings behind the lacquered
brass tendons of his cage
are a pathetic fallacy,

raking away the cosmetics
of grouped vinyl chairs –
the plants arranged like
a high wax finish.

He sings into his striped
shadows of the sun,
as a wheelchair whispers
spokes down the hall.

THE DOLL

Rouge the cracked china of her cheeks.
Tie a pink ribbon in her hair.
Dress up the ninety-year-old
for a visit from her relatives.

And we come in and sit beside her,
uncomfortable at the living funeral.
She says, "Oh yes. Yes," to everything;
but her eyes fold us back gently,
pale as tissue paper.

Hidden behind the bedroom door, she
snips gold fringe from her mother's earrings,
to make a necklace for her doll's
Limoges white neck.

She strokes the ribbon in her hair
and smiles tenderly at the wall.
We leave. Flat white shoes
put her away unbroken.

THE VISIT

The wild-animal fear is upon him.
Still young enough to smell
death and the cripple,
he does not want to come in
here where she lies in her crib.
But he does – guarded by the lives

of grandmother and mother,
eyes strafing the room for comfort.
Her witch-aged face turns.
The tendon-raw hands reach through the bars.
Time is a membrane between their touch.
"My baby, my baby boy," she says,
pulling him into her parenthesis of steel.
"You must not call him a baby," we reprimand.
His voice is torn linen; "She can call me anything."

Could he be the face?
She laughs at us and kisses
his hair through the cage.

The Portrait

He wouldn't buy her shoes
because her family was rich.

So she washed the curds
out of the milk bottles –
love clung a sour white scab on glass –

and took the bottles back to the dairy
saving the pennies for cheap shoes.

It was only after she was crippled
that she came home on carbuncled feet,
to live again with her brothers and sisters

in the house where the prairie wind
sloughed the last scent off the roses.

She painted their roses on their plates;
for their dining-room wall, in another frame,
blue ripples of grapes falling into their own shadows

on a tablecloth –
bloom on china – ripeness on canvas.

And again and again she painted herself,
not in a palette of poses, but always
quarter-profile against a ringent background;

only shoulders and a fracture of a face,
just enough to be someone you almost knew.

When he died in a telegram
she painted herself quarter-view again –
a portrait of a woman as less than one.

Moon Walk

My son lies a monochrome of the moon –
the moon that throws the window on the floor
marking a pale path of stepping-stones.

I walk through her window to his bedside.
She has crawled into even
the small curl of his hands, coating him,
as mercury does gold, with her light.

And though we spin under her light;
a small blue gall smudged with continents,
wearing a ragged shawl of cloud,

the moon is printed with our fate –
apron stringed to us now by more
than the fishhook drag of tides.

She slips over the small corner of my clay.
Her cool alloy clings to his cheek
as I walk through her window
leaving no mark on this side of space.

The Death of a Photographer

Light was his paradigm:
he wove it, a cat's cradle
to knot them in, eyes rounded
to the dead instant on paper –
an 8 × 10 moment – glossy.

It was a trade of stealth,
the black box a trap
for the unstilted gesture;
and maybe that is why
he stole things –

ashtrays, wives, and Bibles –
always in need of basics.
He had compassion for the unpossessed
objects scarred by the anonymity
of hotel rooms, never taking the new,
only those roughed with use like
the corroded edge of his pant cuff.

And the wives:
perhaps it was the stealth and
the way he saw them in secret under
the catafalque of the camera's cloth,
smiles buried upside down on

ground glass, a mask reversed;
and still their skirts were neat –
defying gravity. Like a Japanese
who has saved a life, having seen
them exposed, he felt responsible.

Late at night, after
they had left, he enlarged their faces
and watched them bloom blank paper,
a monochrome resolve, swimming from
alkali to acid. He hung them on a
clothesline and left the room
ambushed by drying smiles.

There were six wet handkerchiefs
and one dry that would not
cry here, in the cold silence
of folding chairs.
The blurred faces turned

to the clattering edge of
sunlight and walked into their
own focus, while his portrait,
in a blue blazer, was nailed
down to its dark frame.

Grand Army Plaza

10:00 at night in Brooklyn.
10:00 at the Plaza of the Grand Army.

The hills of the Plaza lie salted in snow,
the barren trees reach from lamp to lamp
around the circle of apartment houses
swatched with lights,

and at the far end, the arch under searchlights
shines its mouth of neither entrance nor exit
against the nighted trees at the beginning of Prospect Park.

The arch of the Grand Army,
an imitation of the Washington Square Arch,
an imitation of the Arc de Triomphe,
imitation of the Arch of Trajan,
which imitates an infinite number of victorious openings;

and if you set them up in your imagination,
a series of croquet hoops reaching back to Adam and Eve,
who stand joined by epaulets of snow
in the fountain at the middle of the Plaza,
they are an arcade of ages
with Victory in her chariot
grassed greener than graves by the rain
always rearing her bitted horses at the top.

In the bereavement of belief more real than their lives,
they died for Grant's bronze uptown tomb,
for Lincoln's marble throne –
in armor and anger, for flags and faces they died –

for the Invalides' concrete courtyard of glory,
for the Colosseum's ancient malocclused bite
against a bright sky.

Snow seasons the bulldozed man-made hills
at the Plaza of the Grand Army
and beyond no searchlight condones the trees in Prospect Park,
where the sky salts a wither of grass.

The Viking Grave at Ladby

An old whale hump of earth
it rises between plowed furrows of a farm,
a memory of violence in these peaceful fields
where only the poppies bleed wild amongst the wheat
rooted in a memory now fallow in the soil.

You enter the earth,
walk down stairs into the tomb
domed in the sun with grass and wildflowers.

And there in a glass showcase,
as though it were ordinary as an earring,
a fossil under fluorescent light,
is the boat and the bones nine hundred years old.

The planks are decomposed until they are only
a child's fingernail tracing in the dirt.

The ribs are broken,
but still the bow of triumph breaches,
a wave forever at the cupped crest,
alone out of the earth
though rot is its wake.

Between its ribs a compost heap
of bones and ornaments –
dogs, horses, and gold –
sacrificed by those who knew
life must be made a gift to death
if there is to be memory.

All the bones are there but his,
the man who was worthy of sacrifice,

the man whom they wanted to live
through these animal deaths,
whom they wanted to ride
triumphant into Odin's kingdom –
heels to horse and hounds to hand.

But when Christ came on an East wind
the folk were afraid
caught between the crucifix and the sword –
between wood and steel.

They thought this man came back
a rider over the sea of eternity
on that storm a pale rider
his hound baying at his hand

to stalk their fields
where his tomb rose among their furrows
a memory of the old belief,
a humped animal asleep under the moon.

Since they had decided to let a man die for them,
rather than die for a man,
afraid of what they had forsaken
they pled in the dark to a dead God

and to exorcise the ghost of glory
they dug the man out of the mound.

While the priest muttered the words against their fear
the church bell rang across the level fields

swallowing its own echo.
Faith desecrated faith to consecrate.

Shivering terror they carried his bones
in solemn procession to the sea
and cast him into the salt.

They unearthed a Lazarus
without a Christ to flesh him,
gave Christ a tomb unangeled
but as empty as his own.

It is nine hundred years
since the warrior was lost in the waves

and still one rises from his grave,
from the fluorescent's pale refrigerator light,
eyes cringing in the sun and poppies,
carrying a darkness on hands and clothes,

while somewhere the warrior wanders
in anger alone, cast out by Christ,
his bones tumbling like dice in the waves –
this earth his empty reliquary
where for nine hundred years
they have grown their wheat out of his grave.

Impressions

For my son

I pluck the leaves and print them.
See. These are the ligaments of life,
sealed from the stamp pad to page,
ink ruts the fluted module of the ginkgo,
transplanted from chlorophyll to pulp.

I guide you through the park
entering these designs into your book.
But this is only an outline
leaf to leaf. Turn the page.

We discard them
their veins dying in the stain of our proof.
And then comes the reversal.
The spore of life tracks us.
It clasps the wind behind our heels,
scraping the concrete with a sound that smothers
our hands in a cocoon of grave wrappings.

As we walk away to that spindling echo
I remember the cave in Spain;
the bison propped against the wall
tacky as half-coagulated blood
after how many thousand years?
An animal of life's desire leaning against stone.
The fingerprints still wet upon its flank.

The Architect

Whatever his dreams have been it is now hard to say,
perhaps to build the last cathedral for an age
watching God depart – the light gone left windows glass –
so that he might say, I have given you domes and altars,
I can praise no more and will not go within to beg.

But the lust that carved fingers round a pencil
has worn down, a chiseled saint caressed into his stone,
the wash of a watercolor sky that pales
into the pure primary fact of blankest paper.

It was so much more difficult than he thought,
not just bricks and mortar but wives and children.
There was no commanding the kaleidoscope to stop.
The pieces kept on falling in and out.

Now he walks his property under lean-boughed trees
where clouds are torn in the naked snare of twigs
and marks for the ax those that could not survive,
feeling the grass crisp with frost beneath his feet.

The leaves curl black over the hidden embers
but he sees above the haze of memory sharp and warm;
the wild ducks in arcs of numbers fly so low
he hears the wind that cries through feathered wings.

The Phosphorescent Man

The smell of roast beef and browning potatoes
grew stronger, caught in the dimness of the stairwell
between the street door's stained glass and
the climb to the dining room, where my father
was a black-and-white unrecognizable child
with a collie above the sideboard;
and the old woman who lived alone with a brass bedstead
huddled in her furniture –
all that was left after time and death.

Her face was a blurred baked apple
surrounded by the canaries' fluff –
dandelions of song wired in the window's sun.
Under the table her black shoes hid
with her arthritic legs
that bloated above the laces
into pastry bags of pain.

But I never knew him because he died
before I was two, before my memory
could arrange him to the trophy of a grandpa,
as she became grandma with a foreign voice,
canaries, a silver creamer, and crippled legs.

Grandma and Grandpa
one sound and one silence,
as light is to shadow, presence to absence,
conscious to unconscious,
fact to the dark nimbus that is not knowledge,
but is fishhooked with questions,
always they divide.

She is visible.
He is the phosphorescent man.

In the Brooklyn house where I first found
I wanted to find him, her silver
was behind my glass face on the corner cupboard.
His books hung in their black bindings
cracking in the steam heat –
Kierkegaard, Schopenhauer, Swedenborg –
behind my breath on the bookcases' glass doors.

To see, to touch, that is all I know of him.
The rest is photographs, a wedding moustache
and a man holding my father for a Sunday photograph
in a dustless curling brim beyond the frame.
Beyond that there are other people's stories.

My father remembers his father,
a man who preferred Brooklyn to his patrimony
of acres by the Baltic Sea,
eating the roast beef in silence,
walking down to the basement
past the banistered angles
while his wife played the piano.

He read before the furnace's open door –
alone with the flames and the page.

The piano far away, compartment by compartment
of floors and ceilings, sang to the wired yellow wings
as the coal settled into ash and clinkers
until she rang him to bed with a silver knife on the radiator.

She snuffed out the canaries
with hoods made from leftover bits of curtain
and covered the keys of her music.
He banked the fire, closed the furnace door.

The clang of embers followed his finger
in its place in the book,
up the banisters' barred shadows as he
put out the lights landing by landing.

I see him as my father tells it,
but I know him the way the artist knows Plato's Ideal –
a second removed remembrance
a picture of a man
a story of a man.

Some people have graves but some have only stones,
and you cannot bring them the ransom
of flowers or flags on appropriate days
because you do not know where they died.

Someone walked alone in his own where;
after the music was over
and the coals caught their burnt out stones in the grate,
he extinguished the shadows lamp by lamp that
clung to the stair obstinate as salt.

PART III

Come with Me into Winter's Disheveled Grass

Come with me into winter's disheveled grass.
Bittersweet beads against the unhinged and barren apple tree.
Inside its gored trunk a last wad of snow lingers.

I give you a burr spined like a sea urchin.
You give me the split womb of the milkweed.

Together we will gather the hunter's cartridges
strewn across the frozen earth.
Red for you.
Green for me.
How their cylinders glow their hollows in the sun
now that death is gone.

The Quarrel

You sit behind your coffee.
I sit behind mine.
Our eyes are inside us.

Silence lies stale between us
on this morning whose heat is rent
by the singular shrill of a cicada.

Our quarrel is stale as a warped slice of bread.
Oppressive as this August morning is our love,
which, mute as a moth with a torn wing,
lurches a path across the table.

Why Didn't Anyone Tell Hester Prynne?

Pity him up to his waist in middle age,
neither celibate nor pervert in ceramics, only ultimate
with a finger caught in the clay cookie jar.

Leading under the slatted moonlight
of palm trees, opening, shutting,
like a nervous venetian blind –
he said shyly,
"Have you ever done this before?"
She said, "No,"
curling her toes expectantly into the sand.
God sighed relief through his gray beard.

I don't know what happened to him. But she went home,
a smug pendulum of skirts, to inform her husband,
who had angelic nightmares ever after,
"Gabriel told me to."

Deception Pass

For Judy and Mark Kawasaki

It is very high here
where the Pacific limbs blue between the islands
among rocks scabbed with gray lichens.

A gray crochet of lichens,
the humble one-celled union of land and sea –
alga and fungus – works stone.

There is a photograph of the world, taken from outer space,
that resembles this rock,
a thing tender in its clasp of cloud and continent.

Their gentle chisel of growth
casts the rock to earth circle by circle,
an expanding scab of life,

and all their progeny are sand,
as if the earth were an ever-after hourglass
with this frail lace the only supplier of time.

This pale marriage clasps the eternal and makes it tick,
makes forever green
hours of trees

forever half-grown in the Pacific wind
where the serene shadow of a gull
lingers upon this thigh of tide.

Love in Black and White

My mouth salty with the taste of your flesh,
we lie tangled – sand and sea wrack.
Your arms the color
of my mother's cocoa,
of April earth
fresh under the harrow,
of all the bark of all the trees
I have loved
stark under a winter sun.
In this half-light of love
my flesh is a pale shadow of yours,
as though night cast a moon ghost –
paper origami patterns of thighs and knees –
my skin a moth wing of your dusk.

But the stain of us
on the inside of my thigh
is colorless –
an egg-white etch
or the glue children use to cement model airplanes,
make-believes of wings and bombs.
Quiet as light you lie upon my thigh,
a Sesame of all the seeds
we will not give the sun
drying to a puckering scab.
And as dawn dissolves our half-light
back to the definition of black-and-white
our mouths meet once more
across the sparrow's waking.

The Nineteen Seventies

The Chinese Laundryman

He is a librarian of laundry
seen through his window labeled
YEM FUNG.
His hair the color of Christmas tinsel
is a tarnished blossom between the poinsettias
that flourish in the steam heat of his trade.

His life is shelved with sleeves and collars,
sheets renewed for love or loneliness.
His labor is to make crisp again
what every day is worn or slept between.

Among the fleshy leaves of begonias,
head bent to my craft, I attempt to iron
truisms shabby as the sheets of love
or to turn the frayed collar of a thought
as I fight the wear of centuries
to make, one more time, the fabric hold.

Johanna Pedersen

Mouth prickled by crumbs of flatbröd,
I blurred glass with breath and desire
staring at red clay shoes small as my toes –
malaprops among silver in her corner cupboard.
"They are all I have," she said,
her English swinging in the hammock of Danish,
"from the earth of my country."

When the milk was warmed,
a comfort for a child's sleep,
she skimmed the skin off –
a membrane fragile as the first
tissue of ice on a road puddle,
"The milkman left you his shirt."

Though we were both island born
she brought a grandchild little –
language and land left behind:
a pair of shoes cobbled from clay,
the altered garment of an old saying,
a voice adrift in a new tongue
rocked in the swell of the old.

The Strapless

A scrawny yank of a kid
trying to be a *Vogue* woman,
I had a vision of myself
developed from the negatives
of fashion magazines and movies –

careful angles of elegance
that never changed their glossy pose
through all their paper-doll dresses,
and the great roses of women
who bloomed like timed Disney flowers
on the *tabula rasa* of the screen.

They were outlines to be grown into
beyond my skeletal youth,
possibilities of women,
a collage of criteria.
And it was because of them
that I coveted my first strapless –
a flurry of tulle
with fat rouge spots of color
hidden in its drifts.

There was a family conference at which neither
Monroe nor the cover of *Vogue* appeared as witnesses.
My father didn't think I could hold it up.
My mother was shocked by an imagined horizon
of her daughter's bare shoulders
and I was forbidden my gown.

In every woman's life
there is a dress that was a dream,
and the dream outlawed gets lost
in the back issues of the years.
But it's there, a resonance in the mirror.
That's why your face is never enough,
only a bare sketch,
and you, with mascara and lipstick,
paint in the women never filled.

Cold Hands
Warm Heart

Every winter Friday
before dancing school
my mother felt my hands,
shaking her head as she pulled
the white gloves of ladyhood
over my icicle fingers.
"Sit on them," she advised gently.

So, in a straight-backed girl-chair
facing the rigid boy-chairs
across the waltz of the piano
I sat on my numb hands
fearful some little boy
sweating the steps through cotton palms
would discover he was clutching the shame
of my ice-boned glove.
My hands stayed frostbitten
through those rituals of romance.

And still in the winter months of life
my hands turn to the season –
twig knuckles creaking in the wind –
as the ice of ladyhood gloves my fingers.

Billy

Returning to the beginning
that is no longer there,
I look up at the gray, stone house on the hill
with its petunia-edged terrace
and face the open account of memory.

My mother says,
"The Blisses are pressing apples.
They've promised us two gallons."
So I climb the hill
through the rusting autumn grass
where chickens used to rummage
red in their feathers among apple trees
split open like winter walnuts.

And memory returns
raw as the pink and shiny skin
under a picked scab.

We belly-whopped down the hill,
the snow spuming into our faces,
bouncing off hidden rocks
until the sled threw us at the bottom.
We lay laughing in winter dust
blinking up at the sun
and made angels in the snow before,
two hands on the rope,
we dragged the sled –
a mutual tail waggling over rock –
back up the hill

to come down again and try
to override our angels to a new mark.

And all the time I dragged the sled
with one hand
the smell of apples grows stronger
until I breach the top of the hill
and there is Eddie, the elder brother,
astride the press ramming the apples down its maw,
while the yellow jackets circle him
drunk and lazy with oozing juice
and the sun that ripens the falling leaves.

The parents, Eddie, and I speak
as though there is
no voice missing,
no silence that has lived
twenty years amongst us.

Then I walk down again,
a gallon of apple juice in each hand,
and stop halfway to rest,
to look over the trees at the pond
where Billy and I took out the rotted raft.
It sank beneath our weight
as we shouted at each other to jump off
and left us floundering
in fear of the resident snapping turtle.
But he jumped first

without a splash one summer
when I was away.
The letter came
to the house where my mother kept her vigil

over my dying grandmother.
I remember the gingham oilcloth on the table,
my mother's voice reading
his mother's letter.
The gingham marched across the table
marking out shining squares of years.
I knew as the survivor I had inherited a life.
The tablecloth paired empty squares
waiting to be filled.

I smell my hands, rich
from the apple grasp of their fingers
as we shook good-bye among the petunias
dying against the gray, stone house.
There are no rafts on the pond.
My mother's grandchild rides this hill in winter.
I pick up the gallon jugs
and descend the hill balanced in their weight.

Ishmael

Fifteen years I have known your face
only now not to know
the face that sex reshapes,
that sculptress in flesh
who roughs your lip with a sooty smudge,
casts your features to her ambition,
and molds you anew to her necessity,
while your cheeks are still soft with my child.

Your mind is in the same transition,
one foot still caught in the childhood glue
of model ships of sea or space
of heroes bland as vanilla pudding,
while the other checks tentatively another world
blazed by the phosphorescent tentacles
of jellyfish and meteors.

It is difficult being two people,
but more difficult to leave one behind
to play forever with lullaby pirates
chased by the crocodile who ticks
a countdown to the alarm of life.

The other self at the slip of voyage
reads in your darkened room
where over bricks and Brooklyn traffic
the wind blurts the sea through your window
as the command is surrendered
from Hook to Kirk to Ahab –
the maimed captain embedded in the self.

Landlocked in my life,
I wave a Quaker handkerchief from the dock,
knowing the ship you set out in
has no oars, leaks,
is lost in space.
But sea and stars are still the same
where wonder looms a white blindness.
Struck with all men's weaponry,
that animal whom we never fathom
turns with us lashed to its flank and sounds.

The Red Turtleneck

Did she put on his knowledge with his power...?
W.B. Yeats

I stand for approval
in my new cashmere cat-fur dress.
A woman friend nods a blessing and says,
"But the bow at the neck must be softer,
like this,
so they will know one tug undoes all."
I turn to our reflections
and recognize the tie of seduction.

But there is another kind of dressing –
George Sand, licensed by borrowed trousers,
opens her stride beyond the hem of her sex.

I pull your red turtleneck down my body,
heating your male odor from the fabric,
which hugs me ribbing to rib.

Whether I put on your knowledge
with the power of your costume
or I realize my knowledge
maled in the appearance of your power,
the core of my womanhood
struts rib to rib in this pullover
as I wear it into my scent.

The Lover

There is enough left, he says –
holding the bottle up to the light –
to soak up the flux of sorrow.
The cat moans in the alley,
one old Tom out for adventure
among the moonlit angles of the alleys.
He seeks what I drink out of existence.

I don't mean women don't tempt me
with their fiddleheads of hair
loosed from croquet-hoop pins
to drift into a down cage about my head.

But I no longer want
their softness under me.
I fear the quicksand suck of lust
so I wrap myself in a blanket of booze
and am self-sufficient in the night,
while Tom tongues the ice from his paws.

Still, I would like a woman –
a high noise in the house.
There's less left in the bottle now, he says.
Maybe she would hold me
as I fumble up the stairs
helped by some young man,
and in the next room
I would hear them make love
as the cold hives about the house
and be warm in that.

I would fall asleep
into the sounds of their love and wake
to the snow draping the window,
absolved of my sex, to feed the cat
come in cold and content from his quest.

People Are...

We find ourselves in the middle of a movie, or, God help us, a take for a movie, and we don't know what's on the rest of the film.

Annie Dillard

We forget some things are only
a summary of their season.

Lilac buds swell with scent
pinch back to death each May
while buildings trellis blind
windows into the sun.

Above the lilac's odor
thick as taffy
the city rises
concrete against the sky
over this temporal perfume.

If it is not true that energy
is never more or less,

never destroyed or made,
always transplanted –
bloom to the blundering litter of autumn
and there is a slow leak of energy

a soft hiss
in the tire of the universe
and it is true that in each
metamorphosis a little more is lost,
that bloom becomes oblivion,

then no wonder we make pyramids
and no-deposit bottles

force the inorganic
into the pose of the organism –
every statue an attempt
at what we may never be

and we are only a series of framed moments
fugitive in the dark –
a Chaplin gesture dissolving
into the obdurate light –
as trapped in finity

we try to forget
                    people are
                                    bio
                                        degradable.

The Daddy Strain

Two friends over a Chinese lunch,
whose most plebeian eggdrop
pretends the menu's Imperial Soup
like a homely son named Galahad,
we strip the wrappings from our words.

Terror is the flavor in her mouth.
The doctors say, "Cancer."
All her thoughts turn ferrous to that magnet word
and she dreams an older man –
frost at his temples but heart cocoa-warm –
to rock her tears and kiss her well.

Out of work, my bag-lady fear
seeps from under the shine of dish covers –
another course.
I want to curl up, a little girl
against a dense tweed fantasy
who'll pay the bills and bauble me through Tiffany's.

Our manticore, composed in equal parts of Daddy,
the well-aged eye of a distinguished Scotch ad,
and childhood's gray-bearded God,
can no more succor us
than the sweet nest of our fortune cookies
can hatch any bird but flightless bromides.

Chador

In a taxi in Isfahan we have no language
only a veil of silence between us
like the chador she holds
thumb to finger across her lips.

Crossing the Allahverdi bridge
whose arcades open and close the view
of birds banking the sunset
we try to see each other.

She sees a freckled woman
hair straggled by wind and
reaches across the men to roll the windows up –
a courtesy for my unchadored head.

When I leave the taxi
I hold the door until she
tucks her length of wimple in.
The chador slips.

Beneath eyes warm as sun-baked plums,
there is the corner of a grin.
The thread of knowledge
gleams through the fabric of silence
as the river bosoms the brooch of the sun.

I Have Lost the Address of My Country

For Nahid Sarmad

"I have lost the address of my country,"
my friend says, her voice soft in her mouth
as barefoot dust on the streets of Persepolis and Bam –
dust baked to the hard bricks of old mosques.

In a bar in Indiana I watch
the square guarded by lupine spires of minarets
boil with a mass like krill before the jaws of a whale.
"I've lost the address of my country."

The night after the women strike,
burn their chadors, their black winding clothes,
we talk half the night, our voices hard
as dust baked to the bricks of old mosques.

I've had no address for a year but car and suitcase
knowing only road, a typewriter ribbon
spilled out over mountain and plain,
trying to find the address of my self's country.

I've felt my life blown, tumbleweed
before headlights in Wyoming or dust off Colorado flats.
I have feared that I will be
dust baked to the hard bricks of old mosques.

I come home to hear her voice gentle
as the eroded profiles of Persepolis whose
dust is baked to the hard bricks of old mosques,
"I have lost the address of my country."

Kathmandu Guest House

Dogs bark themselves
into the dark of their territories;
the monsoon hushes
to flickers of fingernails against my window,
leaving the foreign silence to be invaded
by chords of a foreign guitar. Voices,
from the European hotel next door, rise
singing, in accents varied as saris in the bazaar,
songs of the American sixties.

> The courtyard is a mercury puddle lighted
> by the moon – pearl strung between clouds –
> secure over the molars of the Himalayas.

I listen to their voices, as alien to the words
as they are a generation too young to recall
the songs they blow on the wind,
asking where all the flowers are gone.
I could label today
trumpet vine, lantana, bougainvillea,
familiar names becoming strange in this soil
while bud and bloom remain the same.

> In the courtyard, a ruckus of vine
> crumbles the bricks of Shiva's smile
> carved above Buddha's tailored knees.

I see them cross-legged on the balcony next door,
puffing at the magic dragon,
singing in their prismed accents of Honah-Lee
accompanied by the courtyard cow's lowing bass.

All the time zones I have crossed –
New York to Nepal –
are a series of circling hands
pinned to the pivot of clocks
on whose faces the times keep changing.

Playing Jacks in Bhaktapur

On a cruciform cloth squared in black and white
two old men are playing, with ivory and ebony pieces,
worn as the dust-caulked stones they squat on, a game.
I do not understand
game, rules, or anything else here.

On the other side of the temple square
a Garuda folds gilded wings at the top of a pillar
in this town whose syllables are so strange
I keep relocating them in the guide book
as though their sounds could say the place I am.

Turning from the play of old men I watch
a girl squat before a rough circle of pebbles
with open palm toss
one to the air,
gather in its fall
three from the dust
and capture
the fourth's plummet
in her cupped hand.
By the catch
of childhood
she names.

Two Trees in Kathmandu

Remember, in that garden eastward
in Eden, there were two trees?
Though East, this is not that place.
That book does not even apply here
where a sacred cow down the street
ruminates on mango rinds in a garbage heap
but there are two trees.

One is studded with egrets like magnolia blossoms
preening white breasts among the leaves,
long necks hooked like shepherds' crooks.
The other, right beside it, wears bats
hanging like handbags in the sun
unfolding lazy wings to fan themselves.

But it is not just black and white
or mouse ears upside down and smooth-crowned heads,
but white shawls spread in the sun
trailing whispers of plumes
and black wings, naked, stretched taut;
the bones of flight visible through the flesh.

Where a sacred cow grazes on rotted fruit
bridal veils swoop out of the boughs;
at night the skin and bones of wings stroke
down moon channels between cottonwoods
East of wherever the gate closed on Eden.

FROM *East-West*

Moving

Tenderly I swathe cups in the *Times,*
pack books and shoes,
box thirteen years of life.
Frame after frame comes down
leaving its place.
The wall outlines the emptiness
and with these pictures I pack others.

My son crawling under the dining-room table
dragging a trail of Swee'pea nightgown
to give a cockeyed grin round the tablecloth's edge.
Days warm with the cicadas' shrill
piercing through the geraniums' falling petals.

Some I would discard.

Nights filled with colic crying and no comfort,
with waiting for a man who did not want a home.
Nights spent in a coma of alcohol and music,
trying to find the string in a maze of marriage.

But though I attempt to keep them
out of the boxes
they slither in;
like roaches they need little space
and have lived here long.
They are indigenous to my life,
cannot be left behind with broken curtain rods.
I hear their dry rustle
in the crumpled leaves of the *Times*
as I box my life.

Lennie Swenson

6:00 in the super's smell of Pine Sol
they stabbed him to death
when at 74 he came back
from buying his *Daily News*
with no change for their habit –
the white tile drained pink splashes.

My uncle Lennie who always had a seal
with a red ball on its nose in his pocket
from a Carstairs whiskey bottle
and slipped bands from his cigars on my fingers
to jewel them with a rich male scent
held only the *Daily News* in his hand against death.

Digging down to the lint in his pockets
he came to us, teased the dog and laughed
while my mother provided chicken
until I, his red-haired replica,
waved him good-bye with full fingers, but
on the tile his white hair soaked back to red.

My father moved beyond his brother to the suburbs
and my mother said his laugh was not refined –
a fingernail on the sooty window of her husband's tenement past –
who, one more item in the next day's news,
lay still on the white tile, his pockets empty.

After Divorce

Every Sunday at 9 PM
he brings his bloat
back to the broken home
the trespasser with his belly
Old Bill Cody in his Mod boots
age 40 hanging over his jeans age 16
spewing the dead buffalo
of his ego over my carpet.

He polecats the house
with a stink Lysol can't kill.
The cat and I hackle it a half hour
while we nod and smile
the courtesies of divorce
over the kid who cools it.
When we pay our severance of good-byes
the weekly mortgage on an abandoned house

and a child split Solomon-wise
I lock him out boot and belly.
But he leaves behind
the cadaver of our account.
Faithful to the grave, once again
I bury our dead and turn against stones
walk from the potter's field of the past.

The Fun House Fable

After the mirror of his mother died
he lived in the Fun House at the end of the pier
where the days were soaked in the odor of corn on the cob
and horseshoe crabs dead on the beach.
All night the water slapped around the pilings,
the roller coaster clocked to the top.

He spent his days wandering
through the maze of distorting mirrors
which gave him back fat and thin
harelipped, hunchbacked, clubfooted
each warped him to a new deformity.
To be sure, he would touch himself
watch his twisted hand feel his crooked jaw
and then he made love to the shine of each glass surface
grateful for any reflection.
At night he watched one undistorted star
between the slats of the roof.

When death laid him out in his own image
all the reflections came to look into the casket –
the harelip in high heels, the hunchback in white gloves –
but he could no longer give them anything back
as the sea slapped against the pilings
and the roller coaster clocked to the top.

The Ladies of Lewiston

The ladies of Lewiston
kill spiders who come in from the cold
while dinners defrost in the microwaves
but never tear the fragile tissue paper of their patterns.

In the windowless classroom
where cardboard Pilgrims smile their Thanksgiving
a child in a knit wool cap hunches over her desk
writes line by line down the page
"I am a dumb brat,"
while the other hand reaches under her cap
wrenching out tufts of hair brighter
than the craft-paper leaves in the windowless classroom.

The ladies of Lewiston
eat Babbitt brunch on Sundays
at Elmer's Pancake House
pour syrup over their husbands' silence.

FROM *A Sense of Direction*

PART I

My Mother Left Me

24 pairs of unmatched white gloves –
kid, cotton, and the summer web of Irish crochet –
those pinched fingers never fit anyone.
They are the leftovers
from the clutch and carry of her ladyhood
left on counters,
lost in pews and taxicabs
meant to feel nothing
and leave no prints.
I keep them in the bottom drawer
and wear my hands raw in winter.

She willed me
one pair of pigskin driving gloves
soft with her sweat,
splayed at the seams
worn into the shape of her grip on the wheel.
Those gauntlets her death threw down
I pick up from Buffalo to Bozeman.
They hold themselves loose on my hands
as though hers lie over mine
while I ease the wheel
through turns of fortune
wearing the drive

she left me.

The Rand McNally Atlas

Belly down on the rug
I turned the pages
large and clumsy as sails.
The names stirred
with the voices of ancestors,
Coeur d'Alene, Petosky, San Luis,
telling of work
and the embezzled earth,
Longdale's Furnace, Alloy, Nitro, Leadville.

From the map's homely face,
voices, like my mother's
summoning the cat,
called lost animals,
Buffalo, Lame Deer, Nighthawk, Beaver, Phoenix,
or like children
giggled at their own jokes,
Noname, What Cheer, Truth or Consequences.

I took into the dark,
postcards round my sleeping-pillow,
places that named their pictures,
setting my dreams at
Licking River, Bitter Root, Lone Pine,
and others whose incantation
entranced my sleep,
Durango, Chinook, Ramona, Monongahela.

Selling Her Engagement Ring

You'd have thought her diamond was set in my flesh
it cost me so much to sell it.
They had me look at it through the loupe to see
how the facets had been chipped
by the marriage it foreshadowed.

But I could not wear the purchase of her domestication
for which she bartered small prairie towns,
clutches of clapboard adrift on the green swell of wheat,
shabby hotels which creaked
room to room of harrow and hosiery salesmen,
as she worked out the pitch
for the next Farmers' Association
selling Chautauqua lectures across the plain.

I push her diamond across
the jeweler's glass counter
exchange her bribe for an amethyst
to wear on my wedding bone
to wear on the hand that bears the age spot on the vein
exactly where it was on hers –
her gift to me as sure as the black spot
Blind Pew gave Bill in *Treasure Island*.

My stone lays its bruise
of color on my hand as I smooth
maps across the dining-room table
choosing my route, a punctuation of prairie towns –
Wahpeton – Mandan – Medora – to vanishing point.

Pockets

The point of clothes was line
a shallow fall of cotton over childish hips
or a coat ruled sharply, shoulder to hem

but that line was marred by hands
and all the most amazing things
that traveled in them to one's pockets
goitering the shape of grace with gifts –

a puffball only slightly burst
five links of watch chain passed secretly in class
a scrap of fur almost as soft as one's own skin.

Offended at my pouching of her Singer stitch
my mother sewed my pockets up
with an overcast tight as her mouth
forbidding all but the line.

I've lived for years in her seams –
falls of fabric smooth as slide rules
my hands exposed and folded from all gifts.

And it is only recently, with raw fingers
which still recall the warmth and texture of presents
that I've plucked out stitches sharp as urchin spines
to find both hands and pockets empty.

The Saga of the Small-Breasted Woman

A prepuberty owl with popcorn
Saturday afternoons I focused my glasses
on Jane Russell's D cup in the dark

believing in the inevitability of big breasts
my constitutional right to deep cleavage
that nature and nationality would provide.

But at sixteen my coming-of-age
was a pair of custard cups which
my mother packed carefully in cotton

as though they were a set of incubating eggs
and I nested them in my bra
praying to Jane to Marilyn to all the cinema saints.

At twenty I gave up screened goddesses
threw out the wadding
envied every woman who could

plump pillows over the top of her bra
and took to Chinese necklines, slit skirts –
I started legging it through life:

But with forty closing in I retain the trauma
of the mammary fantasies of the American male.
A pioneer in my Conestoga wagon of womanhood

I search for a man who, gratified at some
quenching birthright bosom,
delights in dumplings at the feast.

The White Rabbit

Yes, Mother,
holding the banister with five-year-old fingers
muffled in Sunday gloves
I did come down the stairs
in my daffodil coat from Best's
in my straw hat with the brown ribbons down my back
and the round elastic that sliced my throat.

Thirty-five years I've tried to remember
what we fought about in your upstairs bedroom
that I've wiped from the inside of my mind –
the house ends for me at the top of the stair –
although I can smell your scent
the bottle with the perched crystal doves.

Dressed in your will of clothes
I watch you pin hat to hair in the mirror
while my small voice hurls itself against you
and a fly blunders into your glass hat
falling into the powder in the pink box.

Like butter on pancakes
the sun melts on the front porch.
I unlatch the hutch
peel the white cotton from my hands
and beat the rabbit to death,
that plump passivity of flesh
soft as your talcumed thighs.

When you discovered the rabbit
your hand snaked the dog chain round my legs

each blow winding and unwinding pain
on the bobbin of my scream.
You beat the badness from your doll.
I wished you dead.

But I kept my secret even while
I carried the cigar box
to your chant of accusations.
All those words have dissolved
into the swamp gas of nightmares.

Twenty years later
you apologized in the car,
said it couldn't have been just me,
must have been all of us
picking it up by the ears –
a hemorrhage.
I listened but didn't confess.
You, eyes taut to the road,
never mentioned the whipping
and I, now that you're dead
just as I wanted you to be,
come back to climb the stairs.

Like a Henry Moore Statue

Like a Henry Moore statue
I've a zero at my middle.
When my son was small
he watched birds through it
or rested his chin on its ledge
when he was tired.

That emptiness is my mother's legacy –
the place her love belonged,
but too busy patching herself
she had no leftovers to stopper me.

My analyst worries about it,
tells me I must fill it in,
as though I were a problem in land reclamation.

I've tried beer and men,
but the morning after it's as though
all the Ballantine rings dissolved to one
and the men just leap through
like fancy horses at the circus.

Considering it now, my porthole of loneliness,
so virgin not even a spider
has been known to lay its web across,

I've been thinking,
since it shows no sign of healing over,
next Mother's Day I'll buy a trailing geranium,
a Martha Washington perhaps,
and suspend it in my opening.

Spring's Nebraska

Spring's Nebraska
is no eyelet damsel but a bawd
who snaps her garter
high inside her kick.
At her saloon
you drink a wine
that's ripe as hung meat
with the stink of skunk and cow manure.
Her fields are green
as con men's emeralds
where pheasants strut their bronze tails
beside demure church-going hens and
eye the sunset and narcissus
red for red.
Gunslinger-silent
snakes thaw out their mosaic coils
for rabbits chaste as their lily ears.
Into these brazen acres
like chamber music in a bawdy house
songs of meadowlarks
fall from the sky
to drop rock crystal
prisms through the air.

Sarah's Monsters

There is an entire row of monsters lined up
like ripening tomatoes
on Sarah's windowsill.
Most of us have one who,
beneath the disguise
of the grotesque, wears our features –
a little man with rat's teeth
or a one-eyed fetal dwarf
gagged with pale membrane.
They sit beside us
in offices or at parties
quietly as disciplined children.

Sarah casts them from an alloy of realities:
anatomy borrowed from her mirror,
deformities from the malocclusions of the soul.
In clay, wax, metals,
they look out at long shadows on the lawn
where she's hung a dead robin
upside down from the chinaberry bush.
Its legs are yellow and straight
as a schoolgirl's stockings.

She clips the legs off
with kitchen shears,
fits them to her monster's stumps.
It spreads cloisonné wings –
enameled fans –
beneath sky, scratched raw by jetstreams
in the setting sun.
From the steps

of her Nebraska house,
Sarah glides its wings,
boned like her arm
that raises our fear to flight,
across the front lawn's shadows.

Good-Bye Dorothy Gayle

THE ROAD TO BUFFALO

Take all her belongings
lay them on the ground in two lines –
a corridor of ownership:
demitasse, embroidered guest towels,
the sterling iced-tea sippers.
Build a fire at the end.

Assemble the women of your tribe in two files.
Dressed in your mother's clothes
walk down the path of possessions
giving into the shadows of hands
those things you choose not to own;
gather into your arms what you desire.

At the fire strip off her clothing;
cast it into the flame.
Take into your arms your possessions
and walk, naked, into the dark yourself.
                    (Adapted from an African ritual)

    They are stacked in the downstairs hall
    each box labeled in my mind –
    china for charity
    wedding gown to the museum;
    the gold sari she kept rolled up twenty years
    will be made into my evening gown.

    Purple vetch in stained-glass swatches –
    daisies cream the field

on either side of the New York Thruway
all the way to Buffalo
but the sky is still small and comfortable
as a blind kitten's eye.

I grew up on Mercator in the kitchen:
a flat projection of maps on which she blazed in red
every trip she ever made
until Europe and America veined
the bloodlines of her journeys.

And yet she wept over the phone,
"He says I can't drive to Fargo,
that I belong here cooking for him,"
my kid-gloved mother
who drew on pigskin in the car
and drove with her knuckles.

OVER THE MACKINAC

> There were several roads nearby, but it did not take her long to find
> the one paved with yellow brick. Within a short time she was walking
> briskly toward the Emerald City, her silver shoes tinkling merrily on
> the hard, yellow roadbed.
>
> L. Frank Baum, *The Wonderful Wizard of Oz*

She always wanted to be Dorothy Gayle –
adventurous and decorous
knowing how to talk to both lions and princesses –
but men were not as easily defeated
as wizards and gnome kings.

My dear, dead Dorothy Gayle,
a pheasant clatters overhead

like a broken sandalwood fan.
The sky is beginning to open
and clouds lay lakes of shadow on the road
as I drive them shore to shore.

6 AM in motels decorated with dawn,
instant coffee in water glasses,
her hands firm through the morning lap
of red-brick towns while I tracked us –
I read maps long before I read novels.

On this road
going up the Peninsula
the rain was so heavy
she had to open the passenger door
to guide me to the Mackinac bridge.

I hear her voice through the rain,
"Don't. Don't ever marry again.
They don't let you breathe."

The world blooms on either side of the road
two springs after her death as I drive our old route.
Wild white iris ghosts the ditches
and beyond the simple petals of wild rose,
rainbows of lupine.

Tears sit on my lower lids
like birds on a telephone wire.
I drive through them
over the Mackinac's high span,
sailboats like dropped handkerchiefs below me.

ST. CLOUD, MINNESOTA

> *... it is the recognition that human life cannot, after all, be subsumed*
> *within nature's annual course which, along with that affirmation of*
> *nature's sympathy for man, defines the pastoral elegist's vision of death.*
>
> Ellen Z. Lambert, *Placing Sorrow*

A small square with elms
trying to reduce the sky
to a manageable portion,
a bandstand baroque in its wooden Victorian swags.
The children are muted on swings;
couples stroll in each other's arms;
a man, belly billowing over his belt,
drinks his beer to Sousa's beat;
a woman next to him knits in time.

"I told you," says a boy beside the swings
in the growing darkness swooped by bats,
"we're stronger than them
'cause girls have to have babies."

She taught me to curl a dandelion
by splitting the stem
and pushing my tongue against the bitter fork
until green ringlets came in my spit.

Her face like a withered viburnum against the pillow –
"Why are men so mean?
That young woman next door works all day
and then she cooks and cleans."
"She doesn't have to, Mother."
"But she does. She has to."

HOME TO FARGO

> *Mortals live by mutual interchange.*
> *One breed increases by another's decrease.*
> *The generations of living things pass*
> *in swift succession, and like runners in a race*
> *they hand on the torch of life.*
>
> Lucretius, *De Rerum Natura*

The Powers Hotel in Fargo
Utrillo print of a country church in snow,
the dead eye of a TV,
a poison-green bedstead,
a man down the hall calls out –
you can smell the booze even in the hall –
"I just wanna li'l luvin'."

I call the rectory.
A priestly voice humorless as lard on bread says,
"Take 81 to the road marked Dead End; turn left.
It's a dirt track."

There's a storm watch.
As I leave the hotel by the back door
the wind chatters the chandeliers
like some memory of chaperons' tongues
dusty now as the darkened ballroom.

We drove – mother and grandmother –
propping his drowsy head between us
as we sang him to sleep,
two harsh-voiced women off-key,
"Row, row, the bear went over,
Casey would waltz but don't go near the water,"
until he slept between the steering years of our arms.

A Jewish cemetery, then Holy Cross.
We're off the highway and next door to the airport.
Two firs and a dying elm
watch over the Lugars and Trautmans –
Dorothy 1900–1976.
Across the road a field
already fermenting with summer heat
furrows straight to the horizon.

I walk the ditch beside it gathering a bouquet:
white heads of yarrow
because it has followed me along the whole route,
a stem of wheat for bread,
a foxtail because it is a redheaded weed,
dame's rocket for beauty,
meadow anemone because it heals wounds.
Thunder boils in the dark massings of cloud
rolling down the openness it possesses.
I lay the flowers on her name.

Mother, I have to leave now,
drive to the next time zone.

PART II

Dinosaur National

Jewelers,
in goggles and buttercup hard hats,
chip out a cameo of dinosaur bones –
vertebrae necklaces,
pelvic abstracts,
a baby stegosaurus skull
like a Disney dragon.
The entire mountain's flank
is chiseled out,
a bas-relief
of rainy-day deaths on a sandbar
long before
the bingo card of our genes filled up.
Big in the hips herself,
it's not surprising
that earth would remember these.
But like a sentimental woman
who hoards
old dance cards
and ribbons from corsages,
she'll keep a feather
or the baby starfish
of a waterbird's footprint
one hundred fifty million years.
As I have treasured
the whorls of my son's day-old toes,
printed on his birth certificate,
so she preserved
four million years
two journeys taken on the same day
at Laetoli –

the long scratch
of a millipede's furrow in the dust
and a human romp of family
footprints, as they passed in the ashes.

The Diorama Painter at the Museum
of Natural History

His enormous hands,
with fingers long and white
            as skeletons of polar bear paws,
work back from real earth
and plants posed in the foreground
toward the perspective of
distance and illusion.

Off the twilight corridors
the windows open their unenterable dreams
onto landscapes that seem
to a city child's eye
melodramas of color and contour –
behind a stuffed cougar
with one kit
the long perspective falls away
to badlands melting
            layers of ice-cream cake colors.
These scenes
perfect, unreal, and absolutely true
as rooms bright behind footlights
the wise child, knowing neither place,
believes.

At the end of his life
he left two windows for the children,
never seen but heard scampering
in the halls like squirrels
            over drifted leaves in the park:

beyond a fox's night eyes –
his mouth a warbonnet of chicken feathers –
the moon-lined pitch
of the farmhouse gable where
            we all lie ignorant of the scenes
dwelling outside our sleep in darkness;

in a tall, narrow window
down the hall,
a sequoia, the base a dressmaker's dummy
of real bark over wire, soars to the one
dimension of his craft,
            the perspective of the whole tree –
500 years of growth rings into 6 feet –
as violently foreshortened as a life.

Josie Morris

Beyond the petroglyph,
a child's greasy handprint on the rock,
the wind scuffs up red dust
along the road that bucks
and sidewinds
the hogback's barren ridges.
It dead-ends at boarded windows,
secret as blind men's glasses,
the sign nailed to the porch.

JOSIE MORRIS

1874–1964

ALONE SHE TILLED

THE ORCHARDS AND THE MEADOWS.

Walking her property,
I make her up –
a small, rawhide woman,
hair a frowsy halo,
eyes large, fishnetted in lines
that tauten at her temples.

Alone,
land and weather were her lovers,
no more temperamental
than other women's men.
She disciplined their children,
raised orchards and meadows
tame,
managed the estate
her lovers lent her
and brought her harvest in

as they were ripening her
to nourish finally
her fruits gone wild and bitter
in the sun.

The State of Wyoming

Perhaps a childhood magic-writing tablet,
which when you raise the sheet becomes blank again
with a sound like pulled adhesive,
after 200 years still largely a *tabula rasa,*
in winter it is a watercolor wash,
a pale prehistory of color
with only the most tender smudges of lavender and mauve
where land rises enough for shadow.

A state of space inhabited by wind, whose dusty phalanx
harries broods of tumbleweed,
it is only slightly scrawled with evidence –
Shoshoni   Crowheart   Massacre Hill
stray facts of pioneers and Teapot Dome
less real than the pronghorn that race
the highway carrying in their heads the dark
eyes of dead Indians.

The clean sweep of land we populate
on a supermarket rack
with male, paperback hips hunched by guns
or on a movie screen's blank
with saucers and aliens
who come,
out of a space beyond stars,
to rescue us
like a tribe of unknown ancestors,
their eyes enlarged by makeup men
to the shadow of an antelope stare.

The Floating Mormon

That summer she hadn't struggled
to support herself.
The salt had done it for her
when she was thirteen
on the Great Salt Lake, afloat
beneath her parents' wind-borne cries.

Behind white cloud-doors,
she saw life as a sort of railway flat
through which she'd pass from daughter,
to wife, to mother,
each defined,
a furnished room in which she could devise

the person to fit that place.
Now, almost thirty, divorced,
and shut out from her faith,
she stuffs her daughter's lunch
with Hershey bars –
bribes for acceptance and ham sandwiches.

Her furniture giving no identity,
she weeps at comments on her graduate papers –
"Banal, your thinking's commonplace" –
asks, "How should I think?"
as if thoughts were dresses.

The white garage doors close
on her last resort –
to be a child curled on the back seat,
eyes shut,

floating on a long night journey,
the motor murmuring
like parents' front-seat voices.

The Itinerant Poet's Road Song

Comin' out of Lolo Pass
the cat began to heave;
the bitch barfed on my brand-new tapes
while I tried not to breathe.

Buy my beer at the pharmacist's
my wine at the grocery store
a trackin' booze is better than
the bars and cowboy bores.

> Willie sing me t' the next motel
> Loretta rhyme me to sleep
> 'cause Bach gave out at Chicago
> I'm drivin' Paul Harvey's beat.

Sixty-five below Livingston
when black ice spun me out:
the stars were caught in an eggbeater;
my guts felt like sauerkraut.

Carton of books just wedged in front
the cat's pan behind my seat;
if my clothes fall in I'm gonna have t' drink gin
just to equalize the reek.

There's a restaurant in Billings
where everything's served flambé.
The lights are low; the food is hot
but they don't know Beaujolais.

Willie sing me t' the next motel
Loretta rhyme me to sleep
'cause Bach gave out at Chicago
I'm drivin' Paul Harvey's beat.

Old Wall Drug's behind me
Little America's the next stunt
a semi's trailin' my Honda's ass
an' a snowplow's drivin' up front.

One lane open on I-25
the black pecker-birds at Midwest
are noddin' for oil in the snow while I
get fourteen cents at the best.

Read my work in Helena
an' read my poems in Crow;
their words are stiffenin' like laundry
on a line at fifty below.

Willie sing me t' the next motel
Loretta rhyme me to sleep
'cause Bach gave out at Chicago
I'm drivin' Paul Harvey's beat.

Had a job and man in New York
but now I'm Denver bound
with a carsickcat, a Hondahatchback
an' Loretta-Paul-Willie's sound.

Repeat anything you'd like to hear
fill in the lines and rhymes

'cause drivin' alone so far from home
all you got is the changes in time...
the changes in time.

Signature of Love

In Missoula, someone has punched
ML L BR into the stucco ceiling
of the motel room with a coat-hanger-end
and surrounded it with punctures
in the shape of a heart,
so that those making love below will
gaze up at the signature of love above.

But I am not making love,
and the only person I can remember loving
is a boy dead thirty years
whose face has long since been amalgamated
into all children with cow-brown eyes.

Under the heart and a lamp
made for an imaginary monastery,
I watch us in the hip boots of our fathers' galoshes
make dinosaur tracks through the swamp,
bend over jello-wobbly clumps of frog spawn
where licorice tadpoles circle inside their crystal eggs
and, as the spring warms, our hands together –

brown and speckled, grubby and scabbed –
try to catch the quick-slime leaps
of what is both fish-tailed and land-legged
among last year's cattails holding up their fruit
like frankfurters on toasting forks.

In the mirror's reflection of motel glasses,
wrapped neatly as hothouse tomatoes,
I know death has made no barrier between us

but bonded with a strength as a broken bone heals
so that I live both finned and footed,
whole as life and death
beneath the signature of love on the ceiling.

Palouse

Chaff hovers like pollen
over a combine.
Land rolls ripe with wheat
and fallow plows dark ribbons
into the hills. Female, fecund,
they belly and hollow
under sky clabbered by cloud.

Before wheat,
bunchgrass,
camas pooled the prairie blue
and horses ran speckled rumps
into the cool gulch's cleavage.
Still, bluffed against the sun
you see a swaybacked souvenir
kept for a child's Sunday ride.

Driving home from a milltown's roundup
through these barrows of hills
the rodeo announcer echoes,
"This cowboy learned to rope
at a California school."

      The night is a mare's rump
      spattered with stars.

A Problem in Aesthetics

They sent him away
from the Revolution,
a child-package to America,
a wooden label tied around his neck,
the whales bumping and rubbing against his sleep.
When he docked
his dead relations had left him
like a legacy to a Norwegian neighbor,
a blond woman, who bent over him
and raised him in a language neither of them knew.

Half a century later, he's still baby-faced
under a gray crewcut,
pink scalp showing like white mouse skin.
A retired marine,
he sits among the beards of twenty years
in the creative writing class
and sings us deathly ditties
like get-well cards
or love poems to his faithfully imaginary wife.

Denying the child lullabied by whales
from Vladivostok to Seattle
who grew up to survive Pacific wars
and love a wife quite faithlessly real,
he constructs his make-believe life
telling us that rhyme and sentiment
are the ingredients,
that art's a kind of almond paste
and trots his poems out like marzipan pigs.

But just as in a woodcut folktale,
beneath the sugar scabs
that he mistakes for healing,
deep within the sweet pink belly of the pig,
a boy's soprano,
clear as red wine in a sunlit glass,
sings of apple blossoms
and we are in a wood
enchanted by a tongue
most of us have never known
and one of us forgot.

Huffman's Photograph of the Graves of the Unknown at Little Bighorn

Taken a year after, in '77,
it shows a slant of bluff
littered with white horse bones –
pelvises like a child's game of jacks.

The men are under the buffalo
grass, the canted sign –
made from a hardtack box –
scrawled, UNKNOWN.

Toe crimped, one black boot
heels into the ground
among the white bones.

> In the lamp and bourbon bottle we share, you,
> whose 17th birthday present was Pearl Harbor,
> describe the graves near Normandy,
> flocks of white crosses –

> "What would they have done," you ask,
> still on your first Survivor's Leave granted in '41,
> "with another twenty, thirty years?" –
> the old scar on your cheek called out
> by shadows beyond the lamp.

> That year I memorized "Adeste fideles,"
> a song I learned without understanding
> the words, and the teachers told us

to put our heads between our knees –
the whole school a fear of slivered glass minnows.

Last year I climbed the bluff,
paths and markers neat as Clausewitz,
read how squaws "cut off the boot legs,"
the *Far West* was draped in black.

I bought Huffman's photograph of
war's bare game:
one black, boneless boot.

But from this height, Little Big-
horn is a wind of cottonwoods:
their leaves, schools of fish,
turning silver in the wind.

The Idaho Egg Woman

Halfway between Troy and Moscow,
she lives in a house
scoured pewter by wind
the back gate a tatter of signs –
BEWARE OF THE DOG – 90¢ A DOZEN – HONK.

In an onion of sweaters,
an overlap of holes,
she complains the sonic booms
crack her goose eggs –
the dog barks toothless as her smile.

Hat crammed to the hollows of her eyes,
their yolks blurred by cataracts,
she explains how she folds
the infertile back into the feed –
a recycling of naughts to aughts.

Snow seeds the furrowed hills where,
a scuttle of arthritis
between the weather of barn and house,
this woman deals in eggs,
her age a cipher of circles.

Drifters: Bella Coola to Williams Lake

Used to being his own listener,
the hitchhiker talks randomly
along 300 miles of dirt,
beard concealing both
face and gaps of teeth
already gone at thirty.
Gravel splutters like popcorn
against the underside of the car
as I drive beneath the blue
pencil-line of sky
hunched by dark shoulders of firs.

"Nettles don't draw nettles
nor burdock, burdock," he says,
rolling his sleeve to show the rash.
Among the raw heads of stumps
the Indian Reserves make sudden flurries of color –
wildflowers in a meadow.
"Sorrow don't draw sorrow,
nor loneliness, loneliness," I think.

"20 lbs. potatoes, beans,
fatback, cans an' a shack,
tho' the rancher's mean –
won't let you have even what he ain't usin'
for your grubstake."
Cattle, gone wild in the forest,
rub flanks against the car;
horned, white faces peer in the windows.
"A semester's teaching in a strange town,
a furnished room,

a lover borrowed from another woman's marriage
is my winter store."

The reddish mutt lopes ahead
of the car's dust,
bones indistinguishable from a ranch dog's
but coyote in the marrow.
Glancing back over his shoulder,
he raises his lip and turns into the trees.
A scavenger, poaching from the corral
to stay alive in the forest,
he travels this road.

Androgyny

They nestle in the hairs of your chest
like puckered faces of starved children
those little brothers of my nipples
tight male buds
that hardened at puberty
against all feeling

just as your hands turned palm to fist
closed against yourself
and knuckled into you life.

These years later lulling you in my arms
I mouth those small fists back to tenderness
tongue them to the male cry
of the woman waked in your flesh
by a female child
suckling her thirst at a man's breast.

The Transience of Hands

A swirl of dead skin,
semitransparent,
twisting against itself
on a schoolroom counter.
What was living has left a mosaic,
a sightless overlapping of lenses.
What lies here is only a memory of movement.

My father's hands
that never stroked me,
only paper
which grew buildings for him –
the supporting arm of a buttress,
embraces of arches –
arthritic now,
wind round each other
like the barber stripes on a Venetian pillar.
There was a boy, in the seventh grade,
whose hands, although they never touched me,
I remember,
as well as the unrequited teenage tears
I wept because he loved the blond
in the blue angora sweater.

I passed from those untouchables
to a husband, a spill
of lovers' fingers,
so that if that harvest of hands were
garden tomatoes
put up in Mason jars,

I'd have sufficient to keep me
through the remaining winters of my life.

But, as hands cannot be canned,
my shelves,
if they hold anything at all,
are piled with sloughed touches
fragile as empty gloves
carrying a slender perfume
of the fingers they once enclosed.
What felt
has moved on to other feelings,
as my hands have too.
Even these hands, so dearly here tonight,
are likely to leave behind
only a wanderlust of touch
as though life were a gas explosion in a tunnel
through which we feel our way,
getting our bearings by each other's bodies.

Sometimes in the night I see us all –
the white gloves of a magician,
a deftness agile in the spotlight,
pulling from air and sleeves
silk scarves, gems, clinquant baubles
until the spot fails;
the gloves fall to the stage with other props,

deciduous as the snakeskin
wound round itself
on a schoolroom counter.

Playing Someone Else's Piano

Touching you
slipping fingers between your thighs
to hold the cluster of grapes
whose skin is frail as 5 AM light –
the stem thrusts hard from them –
I do not know how my hand feels.

Your mouth
gentle as a cat's muzzle at my nipple
your hand
brushing my brusque fur
to find the limpet of my sex –
they do not know how their feel touches.

Holding you
and as much held
each of us fingers a song –
the keys pressed black and white –
yet we are deaf to the chords of our own hands
which only the other can hear.

The Love Poem

A cranky child curled in my lap,
the love poem whines,
drags grimy fists at my blouse.
I push her away,
try to distract her with
a caterpillar's hump on the sooty windowsill
to amuse her out of my mind
thinking that
love poems
like other children
have fantasy playmates,
inventions they puppet
to the actions of their desire.

But she doesn't want that.
A child sprawled on the living-room floor,
she wants to draw pictures
without the necessity of narration or connection,
to make a crayon present for a guest.

A Brooklyn balcony seat,
my third-floor window
looks down ten years ago on a Hopper scene –
a young fireman,
his hair morning slick,
and the blond bounce
of his young woman's curls.
Their voices are lost in the traffic
but the texture of the basket on her arm –
its simple cross-hatchings of straw –
is a close ripple of weave in the May sun.

From my car window last year in a green
corral shadowed by the San Francisco peaks,
a white horse and a dog –
pale neck arched down,
dark one curved up –
gallop together
the wind of their joy.

Having started from Brooklyn and left,
her pictures return, with the last one,
to the dusk of my Brooklyn street
where the windows
make their slide of home
on the wall of darkness,
and she curls in my lap,
content in our lighted frame
having given her pictures to the guest
who says he'll stay.

Wupatki

When a people abandon their town
they take their names with them
but leave their dead behind.
Coming after, we
exhume both site and dead
but may only rename their rooms.

Adults they buried outside their walls,
children beneath the floors
to be underfoot all day
in talk between loom and metate.
At night they lay down with the dead
on the other side of the blanket of earth.

All the rooms we have ever built
finally hold no more
than these bereft of all inhabitants but
a purple quilting of wild aster
and the small bones of a family.

PART III

Towers of Simon Rodia

For Howard W. Swenson 1903–1981

Trapped in a tunnel
of white tile and urinals,
my day's laboring shine
of sanitary rectangles,
I crouch against the antiseptic glare
reamed by the black roar of the train.
It engulfs me
and I wake –
the house still quivering
the smear of diesel horn
as soft as pollen on the night –
and think,
"I've dreamt my life –
tile by day and trains all night."

Air emptied of the diesel's horn
becomes so dense
with orange blossoms
you'd think it something you could weigh.
Stink of bud and fruit creation sits,
a cat upon my chest to stifle breath.
At forty,
more than half life gone,
too late to brand a name
upon my century's thigh,
I brace my arm to wrestle,
hand against my time.

I bend the rods,
and these my arching bones

I flesh with gray cement
round as a laboring arm
whose spread muscles hold taut my tattoos
made from the broken bits
of every day's bright color,
of Spanish arguments across the street.
This chipped and cracked confetti
of our lives
I manage into patterns
on these limbs which curve
like blooms of iris.

My larger flowers
enclose the smaller,
like viscera
or womb-bound children,
or an echo if it could
be held inside the voice that made it.
I built my blossoming limbs
beside the track for thirty years
until I knew,
although I might not finish them,
they had completed me.
Perhaps God felt the same
the day he locked the door on Eden.

Spring Walk

My father and I go for a walk
on the old derelict road
that dead-ends in the swamp
running from nowhere to nowhere –
two ruts almost erased
by scrub, bramble, and gutted cars.

He pushes aside the scrub trees with his cane.
I part the brambles following him.
We both look into the derelict cars,
the safety glass shattered into spiderwebs,
into crystal cataracts –
the cars lie blind in the green forest.

We talk, as old friends will do,
feeling themselves parting.
A rivulet crosses the road
spills into a hubcap
and out again onto the earth.

We sit on a wall beside the brook
where frogs' eggs shimmer in quiet eddies.
To each jelly bead
a pinhead of life,
and in each pellucid, tapioca bud
life circles
looking for a way out.

He says how much the road has changed.
The great elms are gone,

rotted or broken by storm.
He points out the stumps

with the ferrule of his cane,
points out the long bodies
rotting in the clean green,
angry at the new scrub
shooting up where the shadows are gone.

We walk back silent in birdsong.
I part the scrub for his cane
lend a hand over the long bodies
rotting in the green spring sun.

The Highway Death Toll

The highway's edge
of unmalicious deaths
plays counterpoint
against the radio's theme.
In Utah and Nevada,
rabbits' white fur sloughs off the pavement
like the nap of cheap velvet
while I am told Bob Marley's head
is pillowed by his dreadlocks'
tightly harrowed rows.

Great white pillars of plain
bereft of roof –
the columns of grain elevators shade
an owl which,
blood glued to the pavement,
waves one wing
to passing cars
containing the report,
indifferent as the trapped fly's buzzing voice,
that the Pope's been shot
while blessing multitudes.

I did not take personally
the legs of a Pennsylvania deer
that, stiff as fence posts,
staked out the belly
pregnant with death's gases
until, my radio off and parked in Brooklyn,
a neighbor leaned into the car

to announce my father's death,
and I thought perhaps
if I'd turned it off before I might have heard.

.

Forest Lawn

Like an amusement park, the cemetery grounds
are divided into themes.
Gardens of Memory, Babyland, Slumberland
look out over the valley where palms
punctuate the smog, standing on one leg
like molting, Disney waterbirds.

Turned to stone,
Norman Rockwell kids
snuggle each other
in the Great Mausoleum
on an overstuffed marble armchair,
while in the main hall
the curtain is pulled electronically
to display da Vinci's *Last Supper*
remade in stained glass.
A recorded voice
speaks to rows of folding chairs,
to silence as, in the stillness,
sun moves along marble thighs
of *Playboy* nymphs in the nude
who cavort and weep along
the dim hallways of the dead.

Under the vaulting mimicry
of this Gothic attic,
or outside among immigrations
of Italian cypress,
the American dead reside
in subdivisions,
their respectability established

by cloned guardian angels –
Michelangelo's *David* and *The Little Mermaid*
in this park whose theme
is death and reproduction.

Closing Time at the San Diego Zoo

The keepers
walk among Galápagos turtles,
pummel their domed backs
with short sticks
in twilight at
this furthest edge of America
and herd them
to their cement-block shelter.

Looking like World War ii helmets,
abandoned after a battle on the grass,
they wear white numbers on their backs
neat as license plates – 5, 16, 21 –
these who once could not be numbered.

A keeper's rapping
brings out an old man's neck,
the skin hanging in loose folds,
brings out a beaked head naked as a baby bird's,
magnified terribly by those enormous eyes.

And in that skull
hard as a hazel shell,
years are not numbered by the names of cities
or made things like religions or wars.
Memory is the abrasion of rock and sea,
the rub of the two hands of earth's time.

The last one locked in its shelter,
we flock to our licensed shells –
our headlight tunneling

the distance of our vision
in the San Diego dusk.

Apollo at LAX

At LAX, wandering among lost luggage
and children in sunglasses
like flocks of dwarf directors,
I should have known him
under the disguise of an old friend.

Despite the corduroy jacket and prep-school tie,
when I kissed that mouth,
clasped in its parenthetical expression
of temper by the lines from nose to mouth,
as an old Catholic girl,
I should have recognized
the aftertaste of a god.

He stayed three days and watched
the Marineland killer whale
snatch mackerel
from a woman's mouth,
an old man vacuum castle stairs
in a miniature golf course at midnight.
My days were cluttered with half similes –
always the caboose and nothing *like*
to hitch it to.

Until he checked in
for smoking and the window seat,
I didn't recognize him wearing
my friend like a glove.
But it seemed appropriate,
after his other human loves –
the unfaithful lion wrestler

and frigid Cassandra –
that it was us, the Sapphos,
blue-stockinged office temporaries
wearing our ink like eyeshadow,
who were faithful to the last stanza,
where I left him in LAX
waiting for a flight to some other woman poet
among palm trees decked out
in wreaths of another god.

Gardens

In my walled California patio,
alien with unnameable blooms,
and Eastern houseplants enlarged
to Disney flowers,
a wind-bell flutters its cardboard tail,
chimes with itself on another coast
and, twenty years away, rings
from a Brooklyn court
where all the roots I dug are dead,
though I can name the blossoms of that time.

Like sooty leaves that search for light,
the marriage too gave puny blooms
as though it also lived within that garden
watered by the city's acid rains,
and through its time the chime rang gently,
not striking out the hours' measures,
but taking whatever city breeze
came by into the music of its mouth

to peal for the young husband who,
his life barred by bodies,
scrubs at stains of failure
and attempts to tune himself
with the shower's choir
for the young wife, barefoot
in the sun puddles
on the kitchen linoleum,
who fears her husband and her child
because she cannot comfort colic
or his failure.

These two long parted
and the child now grown
move silently within the sound
which on the wind's time
rings these gardens
east to west to east again,
as dead camellia blooms feed next year's buds
or the wind's silence
speaks on this bell's voice.

Surface and Structure:
Bonaventure Hotel, Los Angeles

Four black glass silos
store grains of white lights
waterfalling six levels of balconies,
outlining wired leaps
of reindeer stags that arch
the lobby pool fragrant with chlorine.
Outside, elevators, black scarabs,
crawl up the shiny walls above
pale lassos of freeway lights.

Someday when the freeways crack up,
when the scarabs lie on their backs
in bowels of cable,
the silos, wind-turning
dust devils round their bobbins,
will house kite and hawk
in their honeycombs.
Lizards flickering edges of balconies
will leave in the pool
dry patterns of their vertebrae
exquisite as carved ivory
broken from a necklace.

The Architect

The only places I can find you,
besides the acre outside Fargo
where you lie with my mother,
are the places you made:
the dome you designed at twenty-four,
the chapel on the right side
of the Fifth Avenue altar,
the vaulted ceiling of stars
arranged for a night of revelation –
the birth of Christ, the conversion of Saul.

My atheist father,
I come to your churches –
sit with the dead in a dark pew –
because alive I had no father
under the dome
in the chapel
beneath the stars
just a man corked into his booze bottle.

Beneath your silent dome I puzzle the split
that rived you like a lightning scar.
Were you the man who thought Hitler
right about the Jews
or the one whose mind spun through
Bach's ecstasy of fugal celebrations?
But you were neither a good nor evil sorcerer –
Gandalf nor Saruman –
just the Wizard of Oz manipulating
illusion behind a curtain.

Under the vault of your stars,
I hear you in the colorless despair of vodka
raging against our common lot,
"When I die, who will know I lived?"
Immortality being man-made
as the stained glass of Chartres
that hues Mary blue out of glass,
you are recalled from death by your stars
to those who, anonymous in their devotions,
have never forgotten you.

Before your altar blazing with Byzantine colors,
I watch worshipers kneel,
praying before the beauty of your disbelief.
Perhaps they would find in your paradox
a proof for His presence –
that it is the atheist who
forms most faithfully the face of God.

A Sense of Direction

It was moonless the night I drove my son
to the Fargo airport
after my father's burial.
Coming back I lost myself –
not so much in the streets,
which weave together neatly
as a tic-tac-toe box,
but on the roads of an internal map
I lost my bearings
as I wandered between
airport and graveyard.
Those two male lives which bordered mine,
like railroad tracks constricting it at times,
now follow their own compass.
I drive alone,
all direction lost to the dark
in which I cannot find my father's voice,
although my son's holds my ear,
a fading diesel call.
The wind comes in my window like
the breath of silence where my father spoke.
It is as if the opening of the earth for him
has left some door ajar
and I,
in this vast room of fields,
am shivering in its draft.

The Nineteen
Eighties

A Cappella

Five days of driving with no voices
but gas jockeys and motel clerks
as the radio's accent shifts
from Charleston to Albuquerque

until there is only one voice
in the full Arizona sun of August
where the land is a rupture of raw knuckles
of red abstract shapes turned by the wind's voice.

Like a mother training a child, the wind
has spoken, has said things over and over
and the rock, like the child, has taken
shape under that imperative voice.

I pull off into silence,
into red spindles of rock,
into the company of a lizard,
darting his shoelace shadow across the road

and a vulture surfing the pitch of that voice
that speaks as I would speak
as the potter's open hands hold
earth to the contour of its eloquence.

Henry Moore's Statue at Lincoln Center

After listening to Duruflé's Requiem,
each cupping a dead parent
in the final prayer for paradise
like a candle in the wind,
we sit at the edge of the square pool
where these big bronze bones
will not tell us what they mean.

Across the street at Fordham,
St. Peter casts his net of symbols
to fish men to significance.
But like the sculptures of Peter's God –
these only offer, passively, themselves
to the secret needs of our intent.

Beyond the cast of Peter's net
knotted with reason and justification,
we sail our dead across this pool,
the white paper boats of children
eddying before the bronze arrangement
of shapes which refuse to explain.

Dexter Gordon:
Copenhagen/Avery Fisher Hall

Last time I listened I turned thirty-six
in Copenhagen celebrating among
beer steins and students. Your notes
capered strata of cirrus smoke
until the last one planed across the room.
You shook the spit out and walked past
her self-composed design of longing.
She glowed, an apple tree blossoming in moonlight,
as if globes of notes had bubbled into her
a yearning for you, your noise,
that burble of husky bumblebees.
You smiled and passed.

This time at fifty from the balcony
I watch you making bees in your gold meerschaum,
that generosity of sound
which she'd have mistaken into possession
wanting what was already freely given,
the love making, your sax
leaving nothing left to play.

Yellow Coin

Where the only changes are
from nature's repetitive hand
exposing the architecture behind leaves
embossing the sea's lace on the sand,
we walk in a year the warm enclosure
of her garden walls,
and plant them with our memories.
We find them there next year
in cicada call or wind curve of snow.

But the house I grew in tenants strangers,
and in this city I've chosen for my life
apartment houses with dead and broken eyes
will be composted for next year's office buildings.
Nothing's left of where I've lived
a bride or mother holding her child up
to windows to watch the pigeons wheel.
Down streets where an occasional leaf is flipped,
a yellow coin above the traffic, I walk my flesh
the only wall that holds my history.

Four Windows

I.

Near Grandma's tree-sconced house in Brooklyn,
on a rise that once viewed harbor and masts,
a clapboard house with a widow's walk
sets out a deep lap of porch front and back.
Louvers slant their broken keyboards on the shutters.

Here I grow round eating sweet scraps
of dough from the children's cookies.
My youngest keeps track of life under
the banister the eldest shouts over.
Times under his arm, my husband comes
to have the furrow between his eyes kissed –
so many children, so many chinks
in an old house for money to seep through.
In bed he reads garden books
as though we're a row of cabbages
and he the husbandman, while I read
accounts of solitary voyages.
I wake past midnight to hear silence
in these walls, knowing our dreams rub
them like luminous fish bumping Slocum's keel.

II.

The last apartment house before the highway
on 72nd banks its studio
windows, glazed by sun, to cloud mirrors.

In this room, that light furnishes,
I live with my blond Afghan and my paintings,
large primary-color slashes which,
noncommittal but dramatic, suggest
power in well-carpeted corporate lobbies.
With my black hair cut straight as Prince Valiant's,
my mouth red as a bitten pomegranate,
I meet young men at gallery openings.
Before last night's wakes I apply
makeup and wait. They're like Steuben crystal,
transparent and reflective,
but shattering they sliver your hands with pain.
The Afghan's silky head in my lap, I
drink black coffee, watch the light spawn color.
Someday I'll paint a polished cherry table
with a Delft bowl brimming daffodils
to gild the surface, and none of them
will ever want to buy it.

III.

Leaded and latticed windows gaze over Gramercy Park
where sumptuously clothed magnolias stand among
their still naked sisters in a watercolor
April dusk shrill with the lechery of sparrows.

Does the gray show again? Perhaps I should
frost it next time. Ought I light the candles now?
I might drop the match. I broke the lapis necklace
he gave me on our thirtieth anniversary.
My hands shake so until the second Scotch.
Should I put his cuff links in now or turn the flame
up under Anna's Stroganoff? No wait. I'll wait.

How I fear stillness. We won't talk at dinner or
on the way to the concert, only coming
home – as though the memory of music gave us words.
There, my diamond's stopped shivering light. I'm still
and now I don't fear stillness.

IV.

A crooked nursery-rhyme
house lies in the elbow
of a Village street,
dormers cocked like penciled eyebrows
over small panes peering
at the world which their old glass
ripples to a seascape.

My cat waits, black-and-white,
a fact among the fireballs
of window-box geraniums,
mews down while I juggle
grocery bags and two locks
into the stairs' communal smells
of cookies, fish, and onions.
Tomorrow's the death day of
the inch of life that isn't
harpooned whale or rifled
deer or bayoneted
man, just an inch undecided
as to gills or lungs.
Here where the gables' wings
slope down about me
I ask its absolution.
No priest, no other woman,

no lover can shrive, only life
may pardon me this death
which bitters love. Enraged,
as I when my brother would
dandle my doll just beyond
my fingertips, my lover wants
this inch. I want my life
before I have a life,
and thus I may lose love.
Arched against my legs my cat –
my fact – touches me so quick, quick as life.

City College

5:30 and the winter dark
is bleak between damp haloed lamps
along the Avenue that's housed
both Hamilton and nuns, but now
is flanked on either side by soot

seamed Gothic battlements transposed
and flat-faced modern factories
where the production line of classrooms
will manufacture the raw ore
of immigrants to engineers.

While wind-plucked flagpole lines play brass
to scurries of night-student feet,
I teach the ambiguities
of language's precision to
calculation's latest clique,

who queasy at the equivocal
set sail on their geodesy,
fixed point to point as though between
these lamps where I amongst the other
gargoyles smirk into the dusk.

The Ice-Cream Sandwich

In second grade I felt about him, and
three other boys, quite equally, in a way
the Church identified, later, for me as lust.
He was short and square, chubby in the thigh,
with butter-colored hair. But none of this
explains why I put my vanilla ice-cream
sandwich in his pencil box which was
a work of art, its cardboard covered with green
paper stamped so that it looked like Mother's
tooled leather address book. Its little drawers
housed rows of pencils in all worldly colors.

My ice-cream oozed through levels of his cardboard,
congealing pencils in its sweet, pale soup,
and when the teacher, whose name I've forgotten
asked, "Who did this?" I erupted
into tears, fled to the girls' room
and had to be scolded out of a locked stall
to run a gauntlet of giggles. Apologies
were futile. He knew I was crazy and kept
out of reach right through high school. Even now,
perhaps, there's a man, middle-aged in his
gray, three-piece suit, who suffers from
pencil-box trauma. What was I attempting
to say in blundering, fledgling symbolism?
You melt me? I want to melt you? Was I
a seven-year-old pencil-box fetishist
or an early case of role reversal?

I've never told an analyst about this, but
saved it all these years for you, who,

since you did that bizarre thing during nap time
or in the supply closet
or under the hedge during recess, also
relive the inexplicable in middle age.

The Song of the Mad Woman's Son

High in the chestnut tree
I watch the sea through the leaves,
waiting for Daddy's sail to come home
while Mama talks to the things she sees.

Singing all night she gathers
shells by the tide's white mark;
pale as the chestnut's steeple of flowers
her voice spills petals into the dark.

I go into my room
and straighten all of my drawers
folding my shirts and rolling my socks
to close her song behind the door.

Rocking, kissing my hair,
her arms are locked about me;
good in her lap, I mean to be still
but my body drowning twists, runs free,

runs down the daisy meadow
and climbs the tree to ride
where the wind sings in Mama's high voice while
I watch for Daddy's sail on the tide.

The Mad Woman's Song

My downy head, dream head, sleep my son
safe from the shapes that come from the sea
twisting in foam on the lips of the tide
but leaving no track where sandpipers run.

With long seaweed hair, they snare the children
drown them among the stalks of dark kelp.
Walking the shore by the sea's green din
I gather the white shells of children's eyes

to keep in a basket for the mother
mourning her child, her mouth full of salt, who
follows the moon's path to my back porch
and searches the basket for eyes that are hers.

I'd hold my son warm against my breath, but
fleeing my arms and scoldings, he climbs,
sits among spires of the chestnut's white flowers
and seeks a sail where the squall draws its line.

They leap at his tree like rock-flung spume;
chanting, I force them back to the sand.
Nighttime they finger the windows with fog and
I sing him safe, my pale chestnut bloom.

The Seals in Penobscot Bay

The seals dive in the sun-dimpled bay
disappearing into clarity
and we sit silent in the aluminum boat
as bird-watchers waiting for a call
to reappear among leaves.
Invisible to our patience, what we name
"joy" supples beneath the wave
feathers silence in the leaves.

Like rain-slicked seedpods
the seals lie on the tide-mumbled rocks
and we are still in our silver shell
as Christmas Eve children
in awe of the thing whose meaning
is tacit in not touching
as in touching we come
closest to the meaning of our awe.

Collision

In wind and change
a maple flushed by autumn's fever
discarded scarlet hands into dusk –
a bird collided with himself in the glass door.

The children and I knelt before
that terror in a spoonful of feathers.
The breast shuddered in my hand.
The beak gasped its little flame of tongue.

Giving him a Kleenex box, a washcloth,
the absence of our odor,
we watched through the lamplit window
until he found his wings again.

Tonight, slamming into the glass
of your marriage,
you are stunned
by your image in your son's eyes.

My arms encircle
the pulsed wings of your breath,
as outside the wind deals
a hand of leaves into dawn.

The Vireo

An Adam and Eve in the autumn of their fall
bring order with bramble-scarred hands
to the mildewed roses,
pluck nettles from each other's clothes.

Cropping the carnage of summer's abundance –
black leaves of basil,
tomatoes green or rotting
in rank mats of jointed grass
like marriages that never ripened,
or children who grew wild and weedy –

we plot out a future of spring blooms,
blue pools of grape hyacinths,
daffodils trumpeting beneath the dogwood.
A vireo, come into the garden from his journey,
as though we are innocent of any fall but this,
flutters a blessing about our nettled knees.

The Stone

All day I carry the stone,
the last present of my dead.
A cut-crystal water glass
breaks against it.
My lover's laughter shatters
against its gray weight
into rags of rain.

All day people ask me for the stone,
offer to throw it down a well,
bury it, smash it with sledgehammers.
But I cling to it,
draw my face on it,
dress it in baby clothes and
weep when it won't nurse.

Mother and Son

Still, in the stale cigarette smell
of motel rooms, I wake
if a child coughs next door, my palms
sweaty with impotent responsibility.
Tonight, home for a weekend,
you cough in the next room
sever my dreams and wake me
to frayed ends of the loosed cord.

3 AM.
Turn on the light.
Read.

Seeing the light beneath my door
you wander in to sit on the end of the bed
and we are held an hour
in the lamp's circle
making a reef knot of our loose ends
until we slip from each other again
and, the light turned out,
drift separately into dawn.

On the IRT

A lily in a burdock nosegay,
she holds the center pole
surrounded by other herded children –
two mongoloid boys swing to the train's rhythm,
playing catch with words they mouth
through the subway's steel scream;
two girls, eyes dusty as tenement windows,
hold hands as though grasping inanimate objects.
She, one perfect note in this off-key chorus,
face radiant as a Renaissance angel
with what we believe makes humans most divine,
grunts and squeals and growls.

The young woman with movie-star hair, who chaperons
this congregation of Down's and other damage,
reprimands her back to silence.
Her face retaining ecstasy
swarms fireflies in a jar sealed by aphasia.

Why?

Why? friends ask. Why there? Why not
a deck chair and a vodka tonic
by a Caribbean pool or tours
of Roman palaces in flat shoes?
I want the edge, I say, of white foam
lace on black sand, of curling temple
eaves. A blade I turn inward to
incise through sedimentary strata
of cultural shibboleths, stacked like
T-shirts in tidy categories
of size and color. I excise
an infant never born in my
own country. Caroler of words
kept mute inside my culture's mouth –
omniscient, hallow, awe – she knows
they're synonyms for *rain, cicada,*
rice, star, tree, the numberless
of the numinous. She
incants arpeggios of joy
around the Why? the shrug of friends.

A Colonial Morning Dream

Cocks crow memories
of gardens gone to concrete
behind canted teak houses.

Down alley at the ice shop
the saw buzzes – a thousand cicadas –
cold loaves to crystal slices.

My ceiling fan spins languidly
the last coolness of 4 AM
into the thread of morning heat.

Aun, mopping the hall, sings
softly as her barefooted tread,
into my sweet haze of sleep

a wistful, chromatic song,
which my alien ears insist
narrates the halftones of love.

Sparrows

Where roof-ends rise up into dragons
in the temple quiet of Bangkok
frantic wings are sold in small cages
by women to earn a few baht.

To free wings, to befriend the flight
of even sparrows, earns Buddhist merit
and freedom for the self
trapped in repetitive cages of flesh.

Universal as dowdy sparrows,
in this gilded glitter of temples,
our ideals hover wings in sunlight
to be caged once again in the dark.

The Mask

In open palm the old man cradles his
chiseled characters, names them – Arjuna,
Hanuman, Sita. We choose among
the faces carved to dance in villages
holding out their human hands. In two
languages we bargain circled by
children gawking, giggling at our skins.
If we reach out they shrill from our touch
equal measures of mock and real fear at
the peril of our fairness, a shade for ghosts.

The carver's white-haired wife stops me,
clasps my pallid hands in hers, dark
as the paddy earth she's tilled, and speaks,
not in her language but the old colonial
tongue, mistaking the disguise of my
paleness into her past. I hear warmth,
the urgency of sounds her mouth has not
formed for thirty years. Her voice
flutters in the vibrato of age.
I search behind the masquerade of language.

Perhaps this is a thirty-year housecleaning
of the heart pouring from its chambers all that's
not been said so death may enter. She
stops, strokes my cheek with one finger.
I leave with her naked countenance.

The Landlady in Bangkok

Consider my traveling expenses:
Poetry –
all of it
is a journey to the unknown.

Vladimir Mayakovsky, "Conversation with a Tax
Collector about Poetry"

PRELUDE

What Does a Woman Want?

We read the same books as children – Kipling,
Haggard, Stevenson – and dreamt adventure,
but they went off, the boys, to munch on sago
grubs with cannibals, be rocked to sleep

in a hold where rats and roaches rustled
under the slap of a moon-starched sail,
and on the volcano's steaming lip, pose
for the camera, their calves fringed with leeches.

Coming to adventure late, I'm not sure
I'd savor grubs. I didn't join my Burmese
bus companions when they dined with their
right hands. On a tramp off Sumatra's coast,

I held a scream, a bobbing bathtub toy
in my throat, as two-inch roaches filed
above my head. My bones ached to the marrow
scrambling up to fourteen thousand feet.

I envy the acceptance that accrues to cocks.
They are the universal, catholic sex.
Witch doctors don't ask wives why they've allowed
their husbands out to roam the world alone.

Green with begrudging as a young rice field,
I'm a prurient curiosity,
in my unorthodox sex, to the local men
in foreign towns who hope, or else assume.

They're shoals to navigate with care as I
tack Malacca's strait, round Java's head,
sails spread and bellying to cross the shadow
line, gathering my way before the salty wind.

BURMA

The use of traveling is to regulate imagination by reality, and instead of thinking how things may be, to see them as they are.

Samuel Johnson

Cold Blood

After murdering his father
and marrying all the widows,
King Narathu feared reincarnation.
Perhaps he'd return as a lizard
to be stoned by the villagers,
skinned and roasted –
a sputtering drizzle of juice in the fire.

To evade fate he built
the largest temple in Pagan
on the plain already a hummocked quilt
of mud brick bribes against mortal deeds.

Mornings, he trailed his courtiers behind him
like a child with a clacking pull-toy,
through the dusty bristle of palms,
to insert a needle between yesterday's bricks.
If he could, the mason lost a finger.

Eight hundred years ago eight assassins
stabbed him, then each other,
but still bricks and mortar –
death's dust steeped and kneaded –
stack neat sandwiches.

In his dim arches, where bats swoop,
we shake our heads over his
litany of iniquity, loving it,
wanting evil to be monstrous, mythical,
something our ordinariness cannot achieve.

When he looked down his tunnel's sealed masonry
to the framed opening of light and green,
perhaps he longed to be
without the dark within.

Emerging from his shadows
where bats scream at the edge of hearing,
we watch a lizard warm his blood in the dust
circled by boys,
pouches of slingshots pulled taut
on limber fingers.

The Garden Again

The Romans retreating from the wilderness
of Britain four centuries after Christ,
left mosaic faces laced gray with lichens,
left their stones, dressed and ordered
as soldiers in the rain.

In downtown Rangoon,
a leftover edifice of empire
sprouts trees from its Victorian brick
while a mile away crowds swirl colors skirting
the gilded pinnacles of the Shwedagon Pagoda.
In the countryside,
the woven bamboo houses pour
dust-brown children from window and door
surrounding a church's brick fortress where
swifts skim through windows stained only by sunset.

At the end of sovereignty, just as the sea
gardens a wreck with coral and anemones,
the emptiness of empire fills up,
a compost of leaves and wings.

The Beast

The teak is carved, fine as mantilla lace,
dark with alien iconography.
Rummaging for a familiar shape
among the forms that climb each other's backs
like acrobats beneath the Burmese sun,
I ask, "That carving, is that a beast who's
carrying a woman in his hairy arms?"
Among gilded temples I am told this tale:

> "The King, only a daughter to his name, calls
> astrologers, a colloquy of beards, to
> foretell the fate they read within her face.
> 'She will be seized by eagle talons,' they say.
> He builds a platform far from where birds nest
> and orders guards to shoot all that fly near.
>
> "The bleached bones of ten years of wings now bracelet
> where she, more beautiful each year, strokes sparks
> like crackling stars from the dark of her hair.
> Of course, one day an eagle in a storm sweeps
> down a thunderbolt, and she is gone
> beyond both town and river of the kingdom.
>
> "He drops her carelessly as any fate;
> she falls a dark-haired comet through the sky,
> through open arms of branches to the forest floor.
> The ogre, hunting roe deer, finds her lying
> among leaves bright with the berries of her blood
> and lifts her head's dark burden to his breast.

"He nurses her to health and to his love,
conceals his fanged mouth and his feral eyes
with charms that cast him bright and princely
into her sight, but when their child is born
he will not stand before his son's eyes knowing
there is no spell to hide you from your blood.

"The astrologers, their beards a decade longer,
inform the King he has a living daughter
and heir beyond the river in the forest.
The King sends soldiers. Hastening with her son –
her husband's gifts of bangles gild her arms –
she leaves behind a message with her love.

"The ogre, stumbling in his fear of loss,
forgetting any incantations but
the names of his loves, follows them and calls,
and calls right to the riverbank. His son,
in terror of the strange pursuing beast,
draws his bow and strikes his father's heart.

"Lips twisted to a grimace by his fangs,
the ogre's head lies at his wife's small feet –
who in disgust at this grotesque, dead face
furls skirts, contemptuous, over his unfamiliar head
to sail with her son to her father's kingdom."

Gazing at the ogre, dark in his
teak skin, who never risked the generosity
of love and died a stranger, I remember
my Western childhood also had a beast,
but he did not evade his lady's gaze.

She watched him lapping from a pool and offered
his thirst the quenching hollow of her palms.
He drank, as humbly we must all drink from
the cupped hands of love, to change the beast within.

Hatching

For Daw Aung San Suu Kyi

On University Avenue in Rangoon,
each day she dines on solitude.

Made mute by generals,
her voice is amplified by silence.

A bird eats its cell,
to crack its walls with wings.

INDONESIA

Old women ought to be explorers.

Amended quote from T.S. Eliot

Orangutan Rehab

A circle of unbarbered redheads round
a blue plastic milk pail hoard bananas
in hairy fists, hold tin cups concentrating –
admonished children wary of spills.

On sultry afternoons, officials teased
these caged exhibits of their power, who
became accustomed to three squares, a roof.

Here, after they've been schooled to make leaf nests,
avoid the poison berry, break
the habit of captivity, they're left in
the jungle – city kids at camp afraid of crickets.

But twice a day they're brought bananas, milk,
until they feed themselves, die of snake bite
or the fall they couldn't have in a cage.

Bananas peeled and stored in her cheek,
she holds by hand and foot to trunk and vine
bombarding me with chunks of termite nest.
That ammunition spent, she craps in her cupped

palm and tries again, observing me
with no more malice than my son japanning
the kitchen wall with pureed sweet potatoes,

then sways as you or I did as a child
from the school jungle gym in a daydream.
A sun shaft halos carrot red
fur around her skull as she

selects a path, with long arms swings
thirty feet above the ground from limb to
limb toward a cultivated taste for freedom.

Missionaries

Rusted helmets, dog tags in the garden,
they live in World War II's abandoned purlieus
under the wave of jungled mountain where
as it crests
a Black Widow fighter shines
in the dark clearing of its crash.

Jungle like green heads of broccoli –
the husbands helicopter over it
to the waiting front line of faith where
headmen squat on naked haunches
wearing necklaces of safety pins,
while wives drink tea,
embroider, knit, or nurse a twelve-year-old

through quinine visions in late afternoon
heat tremors and screams of white cockatoos,
until dinner reassures with flavors
from freezers stacked with
hamburger and cupboards stocked
with peanut butter and Spam.

At a bonfire of the fetishes,
husbands stir the ashes of their godly
war glinting with the cowrie eyes of charred
idols, spoils of faith.
Led by wives, a Pentecostal flock at prayers
purls like cramped chickens.
Retreating from ancestral forests to

the neutral zone of Christ, this unprotected
species marches narrow halls of psalms,
Stone Age refugees redeemed from fire
of government
helicopter gunships to learn
how to iron their new white shirts.

Manokwari, Irian Jaya

In memoriam, Alfred Russel Wallace

Dangling rainbows of skipjack swing
from poles on shoulders of peddlers.
Housewives with crossed arms breathe the cool
morning at their open, hill-perched doors.

Calling *selamat* to them softly,
I look from road to the blue, calm bay –
first harbor of Dutch missionaries,
Wallace's fever-misted anchorage.

Outriggers ride, water striders at rest;
the monthly freighter drowses at the pier.
Above, beyond its barren spars, the Arfak
Mountains blue horizons burdened with cloud.

I turn from sun into an apse of jungle.
The path, a century of leaves makes spongy
footing, is hung with bare
thread-tapestries, a spider crouched in each.

As Darwin traced our sandy prints backward from
shore into water, Wallace, looking forward,
tracked our spoor of animal graves to
the future – animals we've sung and painted.

Listen. A pair of fantails,
wings lost in green domes, drop triads
of clarinet notes, globes that plummet air
plangent in the jungle silence.

A bare beginning of a melody which, beyond
the curtain of leaves in the man-made
kingdom, Mozart might have played, a grace
of notes, a little twilight music.

Stalking Lemurs

4 AM, the moon down world is dark
as the river's black volcanic bed
outside my bamboo door. A knock wakes me.
Fumbles of shoelaces, flashlight, clothes. I enter
the night escorted by the river's
invisible sibilants, track my guide's heels over
stumbles of roots with my flashlight's circle
until we must walk without it.

In the jungle's moist shroud, surrounded by bat
shrill gossiping we breathe the dark. A flick
of flashlight spots the copper-penny eyes;
spidery fingers clasp a branch.
Among trees hung with watchful gleams my guide
and I, compassed by our illumination, are
bound by family resemblances
to these hands and faces vanishing
into leaves and dawn.

Market Women: Lake Toba

They've come on board their grocery baskets full
to gossip and shake off the clinging sand
from bare feet and vegetables. They pull
weeds from pale tails of bean sprouts as we land.
These women then will disappear
into their lives. But now I can watch them,
the ordinariness of their day, sheer
exotica. That word's apothegm
is their sarong-wrapped squat embellished by
a wilderness of batik birds and blooms
while we, another clan in our blue Levis,
our dungaree-and-sneaker tribal costumes,
feed their curiosity's appetite,
our differences our mutual delight.

The Bracelet

Two days I bargained over this brass round
of beasts that, breaching from each other, ring
my wrist. A man at a batik-stall frowned,
admiring his tribe's artistry, the sting
of loss in his smile, as he congratulated
me on my low price. Without understanding
the myths, it bought the bronze curve they created.
The Mobil-oil wife guides her in-laws on blue
Lake Toba while the ferry's decibels
of sixties' rock drown her captions on the view,
her news that all the tribes were cannibals
before the Dutch converted them. "The crew,"
she tells me, "don't seem to mind being poor,
not at least the way we would mind, for sure."

The Balinese Witch Doctor

He sits in the circle of his simmering
pressure lamp. (First you must find its private sound.)
Outside the compound's wall, frogs ribbit in the moon
silvered paddies. (Its own combination of
vowels and consonants.) Night after night he studies
the thin palm-leaf books of grandfather, father (because
evil answers to its name), the mantras, the etched
drawings, clues to a new demon generation
of poisons, killers rising from mosquito coils,
the sweet perfume of insecticides.

Under frangipani's pinwheel blooms
(you call evil like a dog) he's spent the day
on fortunes told to giggles of girls, charms composed
to banish roaring spirits from dreams, water blessed
to rinse away witch-spelled insanity (and it
obeys, begs, sits, plays dead), he listens to his granddaughter
sleeping in rough bouts of breath between her parents.
He scours for the demon, labors for her breath,
while on the family altar the down on a headless
baby chicken stirs in moonlight's shadows.

No Exemption for Tourists

A foreign family –
mother, father,
ten-year-old daughter –
stroll through the lush spill
of green, chambered
with voices of grasshoppers and frogs,
savoring the fastidious sensation
of being a unique unit
in an otherwise homogeneous landscape:
the tourist feeling that life
has suspended its rules
and the world has become a petting zoo.

They pause to watch, where the path
skirts the fall of paddy terraces,
darting scarlet dragonflies
sizzle air on gold-netted wings
and figures working around
two mounds below.
The bank is blocked
by turns in the path,
green paddles of banana leaves,
as voices become
more distinct, chiming
in and out of the river's sound.

Rounding the last corner
they come out
at the riverbank,
at the two mounds –
two bodies soaking

through their shrouds
improvised from flowered sarongs.
A woman, snail tracks of tears
on her cheeks, urges them back.
"Suicide.
Girl, boy,"
she explains in English.
The parents move their bodies
in front of their daughter,
turn her up the hill.
"Disgusting," she says.
They chatter the day's cheerful plans
over her head –
a pair of birds
weaving a protective nest of words –
while green rice bends down
to the bright ribbon of river.

Isn't It Romantic

The guidebook promised birds of paradise,
impenetrable jungle, semi-nude tribes,
palm-leaf huts wafting their fringed eaves.

I've got mosquito netting clotted with dust,
large bugs in a cold shower, plenitudes
of naked scrotums posing for my camera.

If I cancel my appointments with
the mummified chief smoked by village elders
and the brine pool across the woven-vine bridge,

I could spend the day on postcards and
pretend I'm talking to my friends surrounded
by village idlers in penis gourds and grass skirts

who pass round the postcards pointing out
the sites of their lives, while loneliness,
a drying rawhide noose, strangles my spirit.

Mother's hand is lost in Woolworth's for eternity.
I long for my personal helicopter to
whirl me from this place I most wanted to be.

Medias Res

The middle's where I wonder why as I wake
and shake a roach, size of a half-smoked stogie,
from my backpack to the jungle. I'm the pale
anomaly, new mushroom species, sprouting
among the women on the bamboo platform
who suckle babies or coil up hair lustrous
as hot tar. In knee-high mud socks, they stroll
downhill from mired Jeeps to bathe. I follow,
slithering. Men heave and haul a dozen trucks
up switchbacks gray with elephant-hide mud.
All day eating canned Australian cheese or
searching for a private place to pee
while idle men follow me in the hope
men hope about all foreign women, I wonder why.

The last truck hauled, the jungle night's quick shutter
closes. The Jeep accelerates its shriek
up switchbacks, headlights extracting objects from
the night – mud ruts, a palm hairnetted with vines
looming at cliff edge, snailed fiddleheads
of tree ferns embedded in this dinosaur dark,
articulate with a wild vocabulary
of greens – Nile, absinthe, cucumber, jade, parrot.
The Jeep stops to let a truck strung with colored
lights like a Las Vegas chorine churn past.
Blindfolded by night, my ears are impaled
by the shrieking rabble of cicadas,
whose eyes are invisible except in
imagination, I wonder knowing why.

Wedding Bed in Mangkutana

In the village guesthouse
it fills the room it stands in,
a statement of human
belief in idyllic desire.

Curlicued rills of wrought iron
are festooned with lace mosquito net
thrown back from its dark, welcoming cave
where the conjunction of improbabilities occurs –
a boy, knowing cows and goats, is
to be patient, tender;
a girl, a childbirth witness, is
to be responsive, passionate.

From this seedbed, despite
withered harvests, children dead of malaria,
on sheets and pillows strewn
with dainty confetti of embroidered flowers,
belief would have desire
sprout itself out of spit and semen,
flourish taller than stunted tapioca and corn
from the same soil.

MALAYSIA

*Allah has laid out the earth for you like a vast
carpet so that you will travel its endless roads.*

The Koran

The English Graveyard in Malacca

Downhill from the roofless Portuguese cathedral
these aliens, from the opposite point of the compass,
lie, a community in the grass, insular
under a great tree's shade by the sea.

Nancy Henry, David Kidd, Lieutenants White and
Harding, Rachel Milne, whose husband translated
the Bible into Chinese – confusing local certitudes –
abandoned by both God and Empire, please

only the wanton grass. A Nissan paintcan is
today's descendant of the vases which have held
a century of flowers for the spirit
of the tree that spreads its shade across their clay.

THAILAND

The Landlady in Bangkok

Because, separated from us by a language,
we find her a character without a plot,
a cotyledon without an ecosystem,
we invent her a husband, in the alley court,
a barren womb in this quiet cell of Bangkok's hive
under trellised vines in tin cans.

We graft invention on observation,
imagine her dispossessed
by a second wife's fecundity,
while she keeps her clothes in plastic bags
and sleeps upstairs on the corridor floor
before doors of the Spartan rooms she rents us.
We pass on hypotheses with other travelers' news –
names of hotels in Burma,
prices of guides in Borneo.

We know she counts herself to sleep with our money,
yet hoards notebooks grinning
with our faces which she forgets
with our comments she can't read.
But her records like our fabrications
are errant gestures around a kind of love.

She has no picture for our words for home
as we've no history for the wheal
of scar raised on her shoulder
when at the temple stairs she
buys piping sparrows in wooden cages

and frees them to gain merit –
each a traveler fluttering
from Samsara to Nirvana.

Fisherman in Songkhla

His mirror shines back with approval, God's
suspense-flick hero. This reborn Alaskan
in his red prophet's beard – the locals think he
may be a Ramayana demon – sweats
his teddy-bear belly between the market
stalls where dried fans of fish fins and drapes
of dragonfly-wing silks are on display.
He mutters Biblical quotes down the aisles, spells
against the customary pagan evils.

For a Nam vet named Jack he tends the gray
rustbucket anchored where the jellybean-colored
trawlers bob in the bay. Told Jack's ship
rescues the boat people, he awaits
his orders tracking little whores who skim
like flying fish from room to room in his
hotel and peppers them with buckshot from Paul
and Revelations while they wonder that
his innocence is as large as his bones.

His God, believing in contagion, proscribes
the houses of all idols. He avoids
the curving roofs of temples and the mansion
turned into a museum where, in shadows
of wide eaves, generations of the Buddha
are lined up in glass cubicles and teak
floors shine, polished by bare soles that lived
for centuries upon the other side
of his white coin of history.

By street-lace of evening lights he eats
his shrimp in catsup, sleeps through softly closing
doors of whores to dream he's fishing, hooking
them from their pagan pool. The women gleaming
in their sarongs, the men dark-scaled, pile at
his feet, an offering to God. The Buddhas
in the museum wear the moon's pale garment,
dream of flowers and incense as they hold their
palms open in the gesture of forgiveness.

Alien Women: Songkhla, Thailand

Sun-blind in the pharmacy's dim light,
I drift between the glass-topped counters that
display modern panaceas and
dried dosages of Chinese wisdom.

Over fish bones, stag horns, roots, I find
almost myself – red hair, myopic eyes,
but Irish and much younger. Her voice a mist
of brogue, she stands, extravagantly pregnant,
a baby's burp stain on her shoulder,

beside her Chinese mother-in-law who
plays twig-fingers on the register's keys.
In this hushed light she's an elder goddess,
Kuan Yin dispensing mercy, eyes dark glints
of pity over cheekbones smudged with age spots.

"Your second?" I ask the daughter-in-law. "Third."
She smiles. "Then life holds few surprises for you."
Considering my commonplace, she gravely
agrees. "That's true." Her mother-in-law's brittle
Chinese fingers count my change.

Both women brought their husbands the rich dowries
of their races' foreign beauty.
They've watched their children building castles
on these alien sands, escaping
from the netted pull of bloodlines.

Together in half-light each is a party
to the coalition of all mothers
without passports or frontiers. I walk
back into the sun's fistful of blades.

Three Silences in Thailand

Beside the Mekong's silt-thick flow,
trees studded with flat-leaved epiphytes,
as a woman might weave flowers in her hair,
stretch the languor of their branches
from riverbank to dirt road
but are soundless in my foreign mouth
which has no name to call them.

In the bus station, she and I smile and wait;
she points to my hair, unpins her own,
spilling its crow-gloss over her breasts.
Among the shouts of children and blasts of exhaust
I twine her a braid of tactile night.

Confined in the pillar of shadow made by his walls,
right palm open, a lotus in his lap,
Wat Si Chum's Buddha smiles from his height.
Lips tranquil as wings at dusk
hover benedictions in the air above.
Knowing only the words for a Christ in pain,
I bear no offering but the abstinence of silence.

Adam and His Father

Adam's father, always a good provider,
has supplied a childhood of unblemished lawns
perfumed by Sunday barbecues,
catsup, and sweet relish –
the only admission of change
the height marks on the kitchen door
and a progression of vehicles – carriage to car.

Adam, at twenty-two, wanders East
where monks robed yellow as October leaves
drift the dawn streets with their begging bowls
and human stinks are quick as rats in the alleys.
Homesick for white bread,
he strums "I Am a Rock" in Bangkok bars,
buys rice from the dark hands of street vendors.

Adam's father sits in the garden,
evening air thick with honeysuckle
under the gentle shuffle of maple leaves,
and reads letters from Bangkok, Rangoon, Dhaka
in which his son writes,
"Seeing hunger, I know I am hungry.
Perhaps what I have always wanted is to want."

Background and Design

On TV in a Bangkok shop window,
Michael Jackson is a video
rose centering a ruffled nosegay
of Thai silk frocks. He shifts

like the illusion of black and white tiles
I changed as a child – black on white
to white on black – from ghoul to lover
and back while fantasy battalions

of fiends sprout from manholes and graves.
America's undead armies dance again
in Bangkok following the snake-hip slither
of the dark General and his incandescent eyes.

In their school uniforms a crowd
of brown young faces solemnly watch this one
brown face, a manufacture made
uniform by stardom.

I contemplate my white against
this background and his dark cross
in America as he shifts
from fiend to lover and back.

Polygamy

"When an official goes up-country
they'll give him anything," she says, this woman
boned like a lark's wing whose feet barely reach
the pedals of the car she's weaving through
the fabric of Bangkok, "their house, their daughter."

She shifts with emphasis. "Particularly
their daughter. It," she pauses on the abstract
pronoun, "breeds a debt the family can
collect. She sang at the hotel in town."
At a light our flanks shudder among

the traffic herd. I see that youthful mistress
smoke-wreathed in rooms of men, sheath her in stoplight
red which cornering like a Ferrari
blinks GO as her soprano flutters mawkish
Thai-pop and rote-learned Beatles vowels.

"My husband, six years later, gave a party
for old employees. He said one would bring
a child. The guests left. The boy stayed." We edge
a gray matron Volvo through the poppy-and-
apricot soiree of three-wheeled *tuk-tuk*s.

"I knew. He didn't have to tell." I ask,
"What did you say?" "I said to him, 'I thought you
were different.' But she was young, poor, had
to earn her living, while we'd plenty." A bus
bears down. She turns beneath its chromium

grimace into a first wife directing
murmurations of concubine children,
cross-legged obedience at lessons. "Still
I can't forgive. Our daughters are ashamed
and the boy, sixteen now, fails school."

I consider, in Bangkok's weave, what landowner,
fields redistributed by revolution,
does not, passing forfeit hectares in
the moonlight, hear the siren rice call
his name green as unreaped fantasy.

Getting a Purchase

Whoring? I guess I thought it was part
of the adventure, that I was smart to get
sex, interpreter, companion in one
package, but by increments of mornings
this brown face has grown dear upon my pillow.

Across the jittering spoons on the dining
car table, I watch her laugh at jokes in her
comic book as we ride north to trek the hills.
She won't like that, thinks walking's for the poor,
for farmers, and now she's a city lady

who taxis, paints her fingernails. Her father's
a farmer. He sold first her sister, then her,
to a man from Bangkok when the droughts came.
The two support ten who, in good years, gather
in the rice sheaves, but never enough to buy

back even one. I paid the bar a month's fee.
We went to Koh Samui. Scared, she walked
the beach but wouldn't go into the sea
above her knees unless I held her. We took
the shells she'd chosen in the sand and presents

from Bangkok to the farm. The family was
polite but formal like a nineteenth-century crew
lined up to meet the captain's wife, who brought
aboard bad luck. She's taught me Thailand, given
me a purchase on the culture, until

she and the country have become a chord
in memory, not separate notes. That body,
each breast sweet as brown domes of the raw sugar
sold in the market, has the softness of
soil clouding round the plow in paddy water.

Two weeks, then I go back to work, to college.
I bought her a diaphragm, urged the pill –
her sister's on her third abortion. Maybe
I can send a small check from time to time.

The Ghost

Woodsmoke guides us through the mist,
trailing fragrance to
the village. Backpacks full of conveniences
Western as our beliefs, we're dead set on
finding these people happy
without socks or faucets.

We wear our watches, digital signs
of contamination
by the luminous hands of time.
Like Typhoid Marys we carry progress to
this quietude hoping
here infants have no gene for greed.

Women turn their smiles, shield
children from our cameras
leaving nothing to record but things.
Pictures of palm-frond roofs will slide on our walls
while serious chestnut eyes
must slowly fade on memory's transparency.

My pictures flash upon my wall, bamboo weaves across
my plaster, conjuring up one little Lizu boy
who, transfixed by my repetitive pallor –
pale skin, pale hair, pale eyes –
wept as though he'd met his future's ghost.

The Guide

He leads us to our village destination
through the stubble of forests stolen by
lumber bandits, past bamboo conduits
spilling water down hills to women in
silver and coral necklaces who weave
on backstrap looms while men tend corn and poppies.
His terminus is twenty pipes a night
bought with our fees.

Rising in his beautiful balloon
of opium above his village,
he is transformed
into an East-West Don Juan pursued
by local maidens and Swedish backpackers;
into a Jungle Natty Bumppo, tamer of trumpeting
elephants long dead as these denuded hills,
and as he flatters us older women,
puts flowers in our hair, he leches
not for our pale wrinkles
but for flashlights, watches, jackknives.

On his morning pipe-dazed path
out of the home odor of woodsmoke,
through the melting shapes of mist
among the stumpy ghosts of jungle, he knows
the culture with the most things wins.

Trekking the Hills of Northern Thailand

The English girl is being sick in the bushes,
helped by the Frenchman.
The American couple are identifying wildflowers.
Our guide is dozing off last night's twenty pipes.

Two pigs squeal in their pen
and the only inhabitant of this abandoned village
comes singing through his nose with a pail full
of corn cobs followed by two blue-eyed kittens.

The jungle's green silence
reoccupies paths where human voices
called each other's names.

Over tattered palm-frond roofs,
over low crests of hills that subside
to the plain's green patchwork of paddies,
sitting on a tree stump, I look out to hills
that answer like an echo these I sit among

and, I suppose, that is all I really want,
the only form of $E = mc^2$ I understand –
file after ragged file of silhouettes,
misty recessions into endless distance –
that there always be other hills.

An American in Bangkok

And the end of the fight
is a tombstone white
with the name of the late deceased
and the epitaph drear:
"A Fool lies here
who tried to hustle the East."

Rudyard Kipling

Perhaps the polluted air
of the city brings it out,
just as strawberries raise up hives
or brandy brings on gout.
A middle-class, rosy, young man,
called Ted, still jet-lagged, knows
why the name of the town's Bangkok.
In a dimly lit dive he acquires
two figures in women's dresses
who blow and roll and leave him
chagrined by remembered caresses.

The knowledge that history's bunk
makes the sum of experience zero.
He buys a blue spoonful of sapphires
which smuggled and resold our hero
intends as his final rebuttal
to prove to his father who's smarter.
But finding they're small, flawed junk,
he hires a threatening thug
who, with refund and gems, absconds
leaving Ted to reflect that the only
honest people are blonds.

Down an alley's crooked elbow he joins
a shirttailed circle of men
dealing Eurasian poker.
The antes gulp paper and coins
of value unsure as the proof
of their booze that burns like cayenne.
Waking perfumed by his vomit,
he searches about for his wallet.
How come masterful, white, realistic,
American know-how's misfired?
Still he's optimistic.

Hybrids of War: A Morality Poem

I. VIETNAM

Shadow cleaves
the cool arcade of tourist
shops from sunlight
as he's severed from the language

of the skin
he shares with buyers
of his ballpoint pens.
A ten-year-old genuine

Norman Rockwell
freckle-faced kid, his mouth
only knows his mother's tongue.
He's a lagniappe from her clientele,

a providence
she sends begging to
fill the rice
bowl broken by his birth.

II. CAMBODIA

Before the rats came,
following the wavering fishline
of her newborn cry,
they found her among pearly slime
of gutted mussel shells,
fish rot, jackfruit rind,
and scabbed plastic in the harbor dump.

Sixteen and solemn,
walled in her street stand's ink perfume
by the gloss of fashionable
faces, as well as *Time* and *Fortune,*
she waits behind the gray
rain-drape of the monsoon
for a face to match her mirror's.

III. THAILAND

His eyes were made green in
the war that built the Burma Road,
littering dead along its verges –
discarded picnic tins.

The road has also decomposed
into the jungle's root and rains
somewhere north across the river
while here he has imposed

the order of his campaign –
a house, hoed vegetables, petals
English as Michaelmas, their beds
besieged in jungle terrain.

Unslinging packs, we rest
among his Western flowers.
Our eyes acknowledge, but don't question,
his within this citadel.

IV. THE MORAL

In a world of face values, what
loyalties have you to this pair,
ally and enemy, which war has folded
into the marrow of your bones?

CAMBODIA

Evilness is a specifically human *phenomenon.*

Erich Fromm

... the feeling of exhilaration which a measure of danger brings to a visitor with a return ticket.

Graham Greene

Tuol Sleng: Pol Pot's Prison

Like photographs of Dutch Schultz which show a slick
haired, ordinary man with unmatched eyes, there
is nothing evil in this face. Pol Pot
is a bland, jowly, full-lipped man.
Murder. Torture. Genocide. The big words
leave no mark on this small human face.

His photograph has first place on these walls,
mosaicked with the snapshots of the dead.
Looking into the eye of the camera
their eyes focus down the well of terror –
a child, his upper lip already slashed;
a man grinning madness; a woman, blank
faced with one tear, clasps her infant.

In the presence of full face or profile
or candids of the stick-limbed forced to smile up
from beds of torture, I move face to face. My
eyes supersede the camera. Obsessed, I
feel obligated to look one by one,
as though by meeting each pair of eyes
I might...
But all I can do is make them into words.

The Cambodian Box

The silver betel box is formed by two geese
nestled closely as a contented couple
in their silver scallops of feathers.

Empty in the shop window in Bangkok
of all but its beauty,
what household of servants and polished teak
did it belong to
before it came through the jungle in a pocket
to buy a month's rice?

The able hands,
brown as bread crusts,
that formed this sheen of necks and breasts
are matched by another pair,
the color of rouge,
which practice death's craft
in the paradox of hands
mated perfectly as these shining geese.

Survivors

They came up to her, strangers in the street,
clutched her, dug fingernails into her arm and
told her blond hair, her foreign blue eyes, how their
grandfather was clubbed to death, their child died
of malnutrition, they couldn't find their mother.
Now, she says, ten years later, they are better.

II

Walled up in the band's riffs of Western rock,
beneath the turning mirror ball that fragments
us into mosaics of faces, we shout
out questions as he watches Vietnamese
bargirls churn their hips. He yells his wife, his
three daughters tortured, killed. He was in France.
We eat our fish, our chicken, listening to
his family's massacre. His fevered eyes
shine black as lacquerware. We holler our
regrets, our horror. He shrugs and leaves us
for deafness in the rock band's restive din,
for blindness in the glitter of revolving
mirrors, for bargirls who ask no questions.

One at Play in the Fields Of

One came home from forced labor to
collapsed bamboo, leaf rubble of
his village, followed in grief a thread
of happy memory to the field
where, with rice baskets full beneath
silken slaps of Buddhist pennants,
the village picnicked. One found a stench,
putrescent stews of naked women
with their babes in open pits. Now
this one's concierge of the bone tower.

Like Genghis Khan's or Tamerlane's
skull towers on the wind-raw plains
of Asia, but cooped up in glass,
this is a library of shelved
brainboxes which look out blind to
all compass points for others of their
own kind. I photograph girls labeled
prepubescent, but am tugged to
the next shelf, labeled "Europeans,"
as one nods condolences.

But eyeless, lipless, brought down to bone,
I cannot mourn mine separately
since we are every one the dead
as we are every one the killers.
The *longan* tree, rummaging
for bloom and fruit in blood-brewed earth
beneath the pits, one day will shade

picnics, banners, children scratching
games in this dust, at play in
the fields of where we all are one.

VIETNAM

For the human soul is virtually indestructible, and its ability to rise from the ashes remains as long as the body draws breath.

Alice Miller

Time and the Perfume River

Small Buddhas smile above their blooms
on gilded family altars, glide
along the curves of the Perfume,

that river named before the dooms
of war ripped Hue's old gilded hide
and Buddhas' smiles above their blooms.

The river waves are slapping tunes.
Greens sputtering in a wok provide,
along the curves of the Perfume,

the smoke of incense. Children's spumes
of laughter rock small boats whose guide
is Buddha's smile above his blooms.

Those years death rode the river's flume,
his rotting incense justified
along the curves of the Perfume

by leaders' greed for power's boom.
War's drowned now in the river's tide
where Buddhas smile above their blooms
along the curves of the Perfume.

My Lai

An embassy's tall gate off a dirt road
is the first anomaly, the second, drinking
tea in a cracked cup, where my people
committed massacre. We walk
to the museum cordoned by eyes
of farmers who live in road dust
as did the dead. My eyes, not meeting
theirs, follow a man, middle-aged now,
once an eighteen-year-old grunt, and our
woman guide, once a survivor at age six.
We move past dingy exhibits,
a straw hat with a bullet hole,
a basin's chipped white enamel, which explain
the dead owned nothing but their lives
whose final moments are blown up on the walls.
The guide, who never meets our eyes, taps
her teacher's wand at each exhibit as
we listen to the glass doors rattled
by the crowd, the windows darkened by their faces.

In a haze of light rain our ex-grunt squats,
tears pages from his notebook,
folding airplanes for children.
The survivor watches
from the steps of her childhood's museum.
I leave, but these two,
twelve time zones out of twenty-four apart,
are bound in working and in dreaming,
in walking and in eating,
in lovemaking and in arguing for the duration
of their lives by what death holds apart.

The Cham Towers at Da Nang

God-faces that once glared at the sun
have weathered to soft ovals and
eroded rounds, which seem to wait for
a chisel to draw features from stone,
articulate as lovers' lips
murmuring in this tower's shade.

Perhaps the lips the couples use
to kiss are the residual
estate of ancient sculptors worn down
by intermarriage with invaders
until the lineaments of their
inheritance are now long lost.

The farmers burn paper money,
offerings of make-believe rent,
to pay off spirits of landowners
their great-grandparents could not recollect.

We

In a museum of the city
once called Saigon, are snapshots. One's
been blown up so we can all see
it clearly. An American,

a young foot soldier, stands on battle
pocked land, his helmet at a jaunty
tilt, posed for buddies as the Model
Grunt. In his left hand he is dangling,

like Perseus, a head by its hair.
Though not Medusa's, it's his charm
for turning fear to stone. Its stare
will quiet, awhile, his throbbing chest.

The tattered flesh that once dressed collar
bones hangs rags from this Vietnamese
neck, captured with the soldier's scar
of grin by a friend's camera.

Is it enough to see it clearly?
We all know what to think. The whitewashed
walls of a second room show nearly
as many black-and-white shots of

Cambodian atrocities
against Vietnamese. No room's hung
with what was done to enemies
of Vietnam, just as there's no

American museum built
to show off snapshots of My Lai.
One pronoun keeps at bay our guilt
they they they they they they they they.

The Nineteen
Nineties

Making the Bed

Her regimen's inviolate. They squabble
because he wants his breakfast first, before
he helps her make the bed, to her a rite
enshrining, as they mutually fold
the sheet across the blanket, their whole union.
She fears he wants escape, although they have
been married sixty years and there's no place
to go but death. She'll show the visitor
her dangling bracelet a charm for each city.
The Eiffel Tower's gold. Hong Kong's the "Good
Luck" character. And this? She rubs the Kremlin's
shine, fretful in this litany of charms.
Names walked off, friends turned into foreigners
beneath trees in the Tuileries. She's awed
that it's insured for thousands while she wanders
in crowds of strangers who once told her where
she was. The captain's tables all are gone,
although a matinee excites her. But
if he wants to escape, all that holds her
from being lost is his hands on the far
side smoothing the fold of sheet over blanket.

The Lovers

Keeping hope in the field of next year's harvest,
he does not love what she is, but what he thinks
she should become. His present is the driest
drought, his love a green mirage whose precincts
he plots out with a calendar of crops
and flowers suitable for the season he
imagines, being her benevolent despot.
She, meanwhile, unaware of flax and barley
rowed across her breast, lies unhoed, unsown.
Counting sheaves, pretending they're her own
harvest, she garners in catastrophe
from the fields of his accomplishment.
            Waking to a dust bowl of unsprouted
            dreams, he finds her barren and love spent.

The Architect at the Edge of the Sea

My stride was two to my father's by the sea,
back arching into its green voice whose final
words whisper on white foam lips. Weathered cubes
in clapboard variations perched along
the seawall. He spoke of St. Paul or Kepler,
of hammer beams, or corbels, footing stones,
a search for structure to resist all tides
while the small sandpiper feet of my voice scurried
to feed along the edge of his.

We ended
at the cairn of sea-slapped rock streaming khaki,
kelp ribbons where we filled my pail, his boots
with mussels. We steamed their flesh orange within
the shields of nacre, luminous against
blue rims – a spoon of moon on midnight's ocean.

In my constructions – struts of syntax, meter's
well-spaced joists – words come back, a childhood language
now tattered in the undertow of his death,
vocabulary of thought which, like weathered
cubes on a seawall, promise refuge, as
though sounds were stones, as if steel structure could
endure the earth's tectonics. Words or sand
a frail shield, a child's hand held up before her
face to hide from a parent's slap.

An autumn
breath blew froth from crests of waves, chilling marrow
to iron rods in my arms and legs. I rode

white mares of water but was no rival for
a lone seal sliding beyond arms' reach within
surge, master of the arch of element.

Word Power

First doll, I rocked her blue-eyed blink in my lap –
eyelashes blunt as toothbrushes, pink pout of mouth.
"Name her," Mother and her friend commanded.
I fanned through two and a half
years of words to find the one to blazon
my knowledge of Eve's apple core of motherhood,
to find the best word my mother'd taught me.
"Dirty," I announced.

The two recoiled, cajoled, and pled a change.
Despairing, they suggested some babies had two names;
but I'd been given one and so I gave.
On trains, in butcher shops, in hotel lobbies,
looking up at benign, pink, stooping
powder-scented faces and their queries,
anticipating her embarrassed smile and their recoil,
I proclaimed, "Dirty."

Akhmatova

The dark stair's colder than the snow-wan world
outside, where pallid clouds and flakes are swirled
before sun's burn. Ice ingots, each stair holds
deposits of cold. Blood frozen into folds
of newspaper wrap, the week's meat under your
arm, you climb to your room's sparse furniture –
to Shakespeare and the Bible, words that wait
for harness – flocks of geese who consecrate
the sky with wings that raise your audience
above the anguish of their present tense.
While in the Kremlin, Stalin asks his spies
where you get the cash to bribe men to rise
and, as your poems speak, weep for their nation,
he who would torture for such adulation.

New Neighborhood

I sold my brownstone windows full of leaves,
moved to where the stern stones of corporations
sun-glower windows down at me. The only
green is the hanging gardens of Manhattan
where terrace steps on leafy terrace blooming
geraniums, clematis, and pastel
profusions of petunias. I'd expected
the querulous exchanges of cars and trucks,
the garbage dinosaurs at 2 AM
which grind up restaurant trash between their molars,
but not St. Thomas's bells jubilating
on Sunday morning or to wake at midnight
in a past century to horses' hooves,
their clopping rhythm muffled in fresh snow.

My Mother, 1930

"Don't worry, Mom," she wrote from Tunis to Fargo
in 1930, "the main street is twenty
yards from me. I'm in full view." Down the hill's
one side a chapel nested in a flutter
of silver olive leaves, while down the other
the town surrounded eggshells of mosque domes.

Alone in her adventure's glory she
sat, hummed *Die Fledermaus* in the sun. Yes,
there was a man, Luigi, an Italian
who called her "golden head," but he wasn't why
she spent four months alone in the hotel
that catered to a flotsam of French counts.

It was to see at Ramadan the park
before the Kasbah glow with "mellow moons"
of lanterns under which men drifted in
white robes, or to sneak in among Chanel
suits waving gilt-edged invitations and
admire the gold braid at the Bey's reception.

Four months' parentheses of freedom, then
the shadows of the prison house of marriage
closed to the limits of the longitude of
a husband, who preferred to sleep in his
own sheets, the latitude of a daughter, who
returned from Isfahan with slides of domes

their tiles, blue as delphiniums, she couldn't
see through pale webs of cataracts. She rarely

spoke of those months I found among her letters,
blithe with her humming voice warmed by the sun –
still happy, twenty years beyond death, in
her secret refuge of remembrance.

Revamping the Virgin

How green the grass looks on the other side.
Why not trade in that shabby, plaster Mary,
a sacerdotal Barbie's pallid bromide,
for a con artist Raven Woman or
swap her petitioning prayers to her menfolk
for subtle growls of a Wolf Daughter's lore?
Suppose we barter her glass rosary beads
for Kali's swinging opera length of skull pearls?
Could we switch the conveyor of God's seed
for a Dakini changeling, cirrus-hopper,
star-strider of an anarchy of shapes?
And, would this alter any of the altars
in the world? Or are these stock goddesses
pulled from a spiritual steno-pool,
bare breasted or in modest bodices,
just takers of dictation? In which case
perhaps we should retread that Virgin, send
her for weight training, teach her how to ace
at poker, raise her B.C. consciousness,
drill her in assertiveness until
she's ready to go back to God's caress
to get it right this time and have a girl.

"That Kind of Poem"

He called our son to ask if he
would ask me if I wanted them,
her letters, for an elegy
because I wrote "that kind of poem."

She ate pills on her thirtieth birthday,
one capsule per lit candle as she
snuffed each year out on upper Broadway
in a dark, soot-drab SRO,
the curtains stale with cigarette smoke.
At twenty she'd cruised on a bonbon
of LSD, a tour baroque
with delusions from which, on occasion,
she'd come back to us. From the beach
in Santa Monica where she'd
slept rolled up in a blanket, she'd reach
us collect, voice rational, upbeat,
to ask us for a loan to fly
to New York. Her rock musical
was opening on Broadway. She'd die
if she missed that night and initial
bids from the movie studios
were coming in. She'd pay us back.
My voice in New York's winter froze
around its shallow edges. I lacked
the courage to confront her while
in my mind somewhere I slammed a door
against the moiling, flooding Nile
of feeling, full weight against that bore,
that vortex swallow that would suck me
down to be whose hysterical prey?

At the Electric Lady she
once, sure that she was Lady Day,
signed up for a recording space
in my, by then, ex-husband's name.
She flew between coasts and ukases
of analysts who portioned blame
among her father, mother, step
mother. Her half sisters networked
psychiatrists, while we, inept
around her, hid the fears that lurked.
I shied from any woman sagged
in layers of old sweaters over
her tattered hoard of shopping bags.
And did we go the distance for her?
When she destroyed her ID and
replaced it with a friend's, already
dead months before by her own hand,
she didn't understand the worry,
the fear, were all the love we had.
It took the FBI a year
to track her down to the clay-clad
rows where in Potter's Field our fear
was buried by the numbered men
who dig graves for the unknown numbered
dead on this island, a small skin
of earth against which the tides mutter.

The parents dead, years are a rind
around half sisters. What survives?
Words not thrown out in exchange for "that kind
of poem" to keep her alive.

Bare Feet

The vulnerable, bare feet of old men
protrude from sheets on trolleys in white halls –
my father's long since buried to bone; now
this elder poet's uncalloused as his soul.
I offer daisies or a perfumed rose
to hold his eye against the hospital's
blank walls of terror, then leave into August's
sun sticky, thick as a white pull of taffy.

I don't mourn death, but what my father's rage
and blame could never give which this man yields
abundantly. Gifts simple as a daisy's
eye, a breath of rose, are replied to with
a "Thank you," a kiss on hand or cheek, as
at the far end of life's long corridor
he exits, blowing kisses. Emptiness
is bearable but filling it brings tears.

The Sere and Yellow Leaf

Is it time to write the sere
and yellow leaf poem?
Cavafy's body reviews an amorous career.
Millay chants an iambic requiem
for lips and arms that sloshed over the brim
of her memory. But I'm not sure it's time
to erect a body-part memorial totem.
There may be yet another who'll twine
with me through the interstices of life's design.

Should he not appear, that hope without a name,
still love's coals will shimmer heat
to be breathed into a plume of flame
or schools of sparks, a paradox that metes
out warmth to cool life's burns, a balm
proffered to the swarm of humans bubbling
by in time. That flame, those sparks exclaim
in the notes of the corner man blowing
the brass flower of his horn into the city's evening.

ACKNOWLEDGMENTS

BOOKS BY KAREN SWENSON

An Attic of Ideals, Doubleday & Co., Inc., 1974.

East-West, Confluence Press, Inc., 1980.

A Sense of Direction, The Smith Publishers, 1989.

The Landlady in Bangkok, Copper Canyon Press, 1994.

"Plato's Cave," *American Dialogue.*

"A Problem in Aesthetics," *American Poetry Review.*

"The Quarrel," *Antioch Review.*

"The Ice-Cream Sandwich," Honorable Mention from the Arvon Award.

"The Red Turtleneck," *Aspen Anthology.*

"Why Didn't Anyone Tell Hester Prynne?," *Beloit Poetry Journal.*

"The White Rabbit," "Like A Henry Moore Statue," *Bennington Review.*

"Three Silences in Thailand," *Blue Unicorn.*

"Playing Jacks in Bhaktapur," *California Quarterly.*

"The Ghost," *Calliope.*

"Four Windows," "City College," "Alien Women: Songkhla, Thailand," *Caprice.*

"Collision," "The Lovers," *Colorado Review.*

"Johanna Pedersen," *Corona.*

"Spring's Nebraska," *Cream City Review.*

"The Moon," "Androgyny," "The Transience of Hands," "The Highway Death Toll," "Gardens," "The Landlady in Bangkok," "Trekking the Hills of Northern Thailand," *Denver Quarterly.*

"The Itinerant Poet's Road Song," *Downtown.*

"Moon Walk," *Epos.*

"Cooper Square," "Night Cry," "The Architect," "The Chinese Laundryman," "Johanna Pedersen," "The Strapless," "Cold Hands Warm Heart," "Billy," Fales Library, Elmer Bobst Library.

"The Lover," *Folio.*

"We," *Georgia Review.*

"The State of Wyoming," "The Idaho Egg Woman," *Greenfield Review.*

"Spring Walk," *The Humanist.*

"The Bare Feet of Old Men" (formerly titled "Bare Feet"), *Journal of the Poetry Society of America.*

"Surface and Structure: Bonaventure Hotel, Los Angeles," *Kansas Quarterly.*

"The Fun House Fable," *Kayak.*

"The Architect at the Edge of the Sea," *Literary Cavalcade.*

"The Garden Again," *Michigan Quarterly.*

"The Cambodian Box," *Mudfish.*

"The Visit" (from "Nursing Home"), "People Are...," *The Nation.*

"Hook and Eyes," "The Price of Women," *New American Poetry.*

"Woman: Gallup, NM," "Farewell to Fargo: Selling the House," *The New Yorker.*

"The Song of the Mad Woman's Son," "The Mad Woman's Song," *New York Quarterly.*

"Pockets," *Paris Review.*

"The Guide," *Pequod.*

"Manokwari, Irian Jaya," *Pivot.*

"The Chinese Laundryman," *Poetry.*

"Josie Morris," "Palouse," *Poetry Now.*

"A Sense of Direction," *Poets On.*

"Dear Elizabeth," "Chador," "I Have Lost the Address of My Country," "Two Trees in Kathmandu," "The Rand McNally Atlas," "Sarah's Monsters," "Good-Bye Dorothy Gayle," "The Floating Mormon," "The Love Poem," "Market Women: Lake Toba," "The Bracelet," "Getting a Purchase," "Akhmatova," *Prairie Schooner.*

"Hybrids of War: A Morality Poem," *Prospect Review.*

"A Colonial Morning Dream" (formerly titled "Soi Ram-Butri Road, Banglampoo, Bangkok"), *Pulpsmith.*

"The Barmaid and the Alexandrite," "The Death of a Photographer," "Impressions," *Quarterly Review of Literature.*

"New Neighborhood," *Rattapallax.*

"My Mother Left Me," "Signature of Love," "Forest Lawn," "Apollo at LAX," "The Beast," *Salmagundi.*

"The Phosphorescent Man," *Saturday Review.*

"The Portrait," *Shenandoah.*

"Dinosaur National," *Slant.*

"The Quilt," *The Smith Anthology.*

"Cold Hands Warm Heart," *Snapdragon.*

"Henry Moore's Statue at Lincoln Center," "Cold Blood," "Medias Res," "Adam and His Father," *Southern Poetry Review.*

"Billy," "The Daddy Strain," *Texas Quarterly.*

"The Saga of the Small-Breasted Woman," *13th Moon.*

"The Strapless," *We Become New.*

"Drifters: Bella Coola to Williams Lake," *Xanadu.*

ABOUT THE AUTHOR

Karen Swenson, poet and journalist, was awarded the 1993 National Poetry Series award for *The Landlady in Bangkok*. She is the author of four previous collections of poetry. Her poems have been published in *The New Yorker, Poetry,* and *Paris Review*; her writings on world travel have appeared in *The New York Times, The Wall Street Journal,* and *The New Leader*. A tireless traveler, she has journeyed around the globe and taught at universities and colleges across the country, including the City College of New York, where she taught for fifteen years. She lives in New York City.

COLOPHON

The typeface used in this book is an instance of Kepler, a Multiple Master font designed by Robert Slimbach for digital composition in 1996. Kepler is not a revival of an historic face or style, but is a new face with elements of Renaissance and Modern typestyles. Book design by Valerie Brewster, Scribe Typography. Printed on Glatfelter Author's Text (acid-free, 85% recycled, 10% post-consumer stock) at Bang Printing.